RECIPES FOR PEACE

Over 100 recipes to promote peace in Ireland

Compiled by Marie Roche

VERMILION
LONDON

This book is dedicated to Edgar McLoughlin

First published in 1995

1 3 5 7 9 10 8 6 4 2

First published in 1995 by Vermilion, an imprint of Ebury Press
Random House, 20 Vauxhall Bridge Road, London SW1V 2SA

Random House Australia (Pty) Limited
20 Alfred Street, Milsons Point, Sydney, New South Wales 2061,
Australia

Random House New Zealand Ltd
18 Poland Road, Glenfiled, Auckland 10, New Zealand

Random House South Africa (Pty) Limited
PO Box 337, Bergvlei, South Africa

Random House UK Limited Reg. No. 954009

A CIP catalogue record for this book is available
from the British Library.

Editor: Vicky Hanson
Design: Behram Kapadia

Front cover photograph reproduced courtesy of Hulton Reuters.

The recipe for Piedmont Roasted Peppers on page 11 is
reproduced from *Delia Smith's Summer Collection* published by
BBC Books © Delia Smith 1993.

A CIP catalogue record for this book is available from
the British Library.

ISBN 009 180949 5

Printed and bound in Great Britain by BPC Paulton Books Ltd.

**A 10% royalty on the sale of this book will be donated to
Children For Change, a registered charity number 12770**

Foreword

The future of Northern Ireland lies with its children. The charity Children For Change has been working for peace since 1975 by organizing cross-community events and providing a centre where children can come together and learn mutual tolerance and respect.

The problems of Northern Ireland have occupied the hearts and minds of myself and my family for several generations. The stories told by my father when I was young made me aware of the religious hatred and prejudice which erupted into violence in 1969 and caused the 25 years of troubles in Northern Ireland. The unending troubles soon spread onto the UK mainland and one violent event followed another. The Warrington bombing and the death of two innocent children in March 1993 made us all shake our heads in despair.

But miracles do happen. When the ceasefire was announced on 31st August 1994, I was inspired to help the peace process and the idea for *Recipes for Peace* was born. I had been exchanging recipes worldwide on the on-line computer networks and knew what a unifying force it was. Cooking and sharing food brings us all back to basics and reminds us of our shared humanity. I wrote to political and religious figures and celebrities in Britain, Ireland, Europe and America, asking them to support the charity Children For Change by sending a recipe. The response was overwhelming and the result is this book *Recipes for Peace,* which shows how much support there is for the peace process. Let's hope that the proceeds of this book will make it possible for Children For Change to continue to work towards a happy future for the children and to carry on bridging the gap between the people of Ireland.

MARIE ROCHE

"From Dublin to Shannon
They all love Colcannon
And no-one has known it to fail.
It's a dish of great fame
And in Irish, it's name
Translated, means White-Headed Kale.

This favourite of mine
Has spring onions, chopped fine,
And boiled up with milk or cream.
The potatoes then mash
As quick as a flash –
With chopped buttered kale they're a dream.

Beat them all up together
Till they're light as a feather
Then pile on some more knobs of butter.
When the whole lot is topped
With parsley, fine-chopped,
Oh, what cries of delight they will utter!"

GORDON SNELL

Contents

Soups, Starters and Snacks

6

Main Courses

18

Desserts and Baking

44

The publishers would like to thank everyone who contributed to this book. Due to an overwhelming response we could not include all the recipes that were sent in but thank you to everyone for your recipes and kind words of support.

SOUPS, STARTERS AND SNACKS

The Cup That Cheers

Take one pint of pure water and boil it in a kettle with North Sea gas.

Add one tea bag from the Commonwealth, some milk and sugar from the Third World and stir until the tea assumes a satisfying deep brown colour. Remove the tea bag and take every hour, or more often if necessary.

Tony Benn/MP

Tangy Rice Salad

450 g (1 lb) cooked rice, still hot	100 g (4 oz) raisins
15 ml (1 tbsp) vinegar	½ green pepper, chopped
5 ml (1 tsp) lemon juice	30 ml (2 tbsp) mango chutney, chopped
15 ml (1 tbsp) sunflower or light olive oil	150 ml (¼ pint) yoghurt or sour cream
10 ml (2 tsp) curry powder or according to hotness required!	150 ml (¼ pint) mayonnaise
1.25 ml (¼ tsp) turmeric	chopped fresh coriander and lime slices, to garnish
2.5 ml (½ tsp) cayenne pepper	lettuce leaves, to serve

Sprinkle the hot rice with the vinegar, lemon juice and oil and mix lightly. Add the curry powder, turmeric and cayenne pepper and mix gently.

Stir in the raisins, green pepper and chutney. Add the yoghurt or sour cream and mayonnaise and mix well. Put the mixture in six small buttered ramekins or one large mould and chill.

To serve, turn out on to lettuce-lined plates and decorate with chopped fresh coriander and lime slices. If you prefer, just pile the rice on top of the lettuce leaves.

Serves 6　　　　　　　　　　　　　*David Jacobs/Radio presenter*

Steamed Green Cabbage

800 g (1¾ lb) new green cabbage	30 ml (2 tbsp) champagne vinegar
100 g (4 oz) butter	75 g (3 oz) sevruga caviar
salt and freshly ground black pepper	40 g (1½ oz) salmon eggs
150 g (5 oz) crème fraîche	chervil sprigs, to garnish

Separate the cabbage leaves, remove the heart and blanch the leaves in a large saucepan of boiling salted water for 1 minute. Rinse with cold water and drain on a cloth.

In a frying pan, melt the butter, add the cabbage and salt and pepper and cook gently for 10 minutes.

Meanwhile, put the crème fraîche in a small saucepan and cook over a low heat until reduced by half. Season and add the champagne vinegar.

Put the cooked cabbage in a dome in the middle of each serving plate, sprinkle the caviar and salmon eggs on top and encircle the cabbage with a stream of champagne vinegar cream. Garnish with a few sprigs of chervil.

Serves 4   *Guy Legay/Chef*

Lentil Soup

25 g (1 oz) butter	1.1 litres (2 pints) chicken stock
1 onion, chopped	5 ml (1 tsp) ground cumin
2 garlic cloves, crushed	salt and freshly ground black pepper
1 tomato, chopped	lemon juice
225 g (8 oz) red lentils	

Melt the butter in a large saucepan. Add the onion and garlic and cook for 5 minutes, until soft. Add the tomato and cook for 1 minute.

Wash the lentils and add to the pan with the stock. Bring to the boil and simmer for 30–45 minutes, until the lentils are soft.

Purée in a food processor or blender (or not if more chunky soup is required) and return to pan. Reheat gently.

Add the cumin and season to taste. Stir well and add a dash of lemon juice before serving.

Serves 4–6   *Glenda Jackson/MP*

Parsnip Soup

25 g (1 oz) butter	900 ml (1½ pints) beef stock
450 g (1 lb) parsnips, chopped	300 ml (½ pint) milk
1 onion, chopped	salt and freshly ground black pepper
5 ml (1 tsp) curry powder	chopped parsley, to garnish

Melt the butter in a large saucepan, add the parsnips and onion and cook gently for about 10 minutes, stirring frequently.

Add the curry powder to the pan, cook for 2–3 minutes, then add the stock, milk, salt and pepper. Bring to the boil and simmer for 1 hour.

Press the soup through a sieve or purée in a food processor or blender. Reheat and adjust the seasoning. Sprinkle with parsley and serve.

Note: For a special occasion, replace 150 ml (¼ pint) of the milk with single cream.

Serves 4

Children for Change is an excellent idea and I hope it continues to flourish.

The Bishop of Durham

Carrot and Orange Soup

40 g (1½ oz) butter	1.4 litres (2½ pints) chicken or vegetable stock
2 onions, chopped	
350 g (12 oz) carrots, chopped	1 bay leaf
grated rind and juice of 2 large oranges	salt and freshly ground black pepper

Melt the butter in a saucepan and cook the onions and carrots until soft.

Add the orange rind, stock, bay leaf and salt and pepper. Bring to the boil, cover and simmer for 20–30 minutes until the vegetables are soft.

Discard the bay leaf and purée the mixture in a food processor or blender. Add the orange juice and reheat gently. Serve hot or chilled.

Serves 6   *Lord Denis Healey*

Albanian Liver

450 g (1 lb) lambs' liver, trimmed	75 ml (3 fl oz) olive oil
30 ml (2 tbsp) plain flour	I large onion, thinly sliced
15 ml (1 tbsp) paprika, plus extra to garnish	150 ml (¼ pint) Greek yoghurt
	10 mint leaves, roughly torn
salt and freshly ground black pepper	

Cut the liver into long strips, about 2 cm (¾ inch) wide. Mix the flour with the paprika, salt and pepper. Coat the liver in the seasoned flour.

Heat 4 tablespoons of the olive oil in a large frying pan over a brisk heat. Fry the strips of liver, in two batches if necessary, for 2–3 minutes, until browned, but still pink in the centre. Drain briefly on absorbent kitchen paper.

Fry the onion slices in the same oil, adding more oil if needed, gently at first, then raising the heat once they are tender to brown them. Drain on absorbent kitchen paper.

Place the warm liver in a shallow dish, top with a generous dollop of yoghurt, then scatter over the fried onions and the mint leaves. Dribble a tablespoon or so of olive oil over the top, dust with a little paprika and serve.

Serves 4   *Sophie Grigson/Cookery writer*

Cape Cod Fish Chowder

900 g (2 lb) fresh haddock	I bay leaf, crumbled
600 ml (1 pint) water	900 ml (1½ pints) milk
50 g (2 oz) salt pork or pork fat, diced	25 g (1 oz) butter or margarine
2 onions, sliced	5 ml (1 tsp) salt and freshly ground black pepper
2 celery sticks, chopped	
4 large potatoes, diced	

Put the haddock and water in a saucepan, bring to the boil and simmer for 15 minutes. Drain, reserving the cooking liquid. Remove the skin and bones from the fish.

Cook the salt pork or pork fat in a large saucepan until crisp. Remove with a slotted spoon and discard. Add the onions and cook in the pork fat until golden brown.

Add the fish, celery, potatoes and bay leaf. Measure the reserved fish cooking liquid and add enough boiling water to make 750 ml (1¼ pints). Add to the pan, bring to the boil and simmer for 40 minutes.

Add the milk and butter or margarine and simmer for 5 minutes, to heat through. Season with salt and pepper and serve.

Serves 8   *Senator Edward M. Kennedy*

Brown String Bean Soup

450–700 g (1–1½ lb) green beans	30 ml (2 tbsp) plain flour
2 litres (3½ pints) chicken or vegetable stock	15 ml (1 tbsp) vinegar
	450 g (1 lb) potatoes, diced
bunch of summer savory	salt and freshly ground black pepper
40 g (1½ oz) butter	

Cut the beans diagonally into 1–2 cm (½–¾ inch) pieces. Bring the stock to the boil and add the beans and savory. Cook for 45 minutes.

Melt the butter in a saucepan and sift in the flour, stirring constantly. As soon as the flour mixture is light to medium brown, remove the pan from the heat.

Slowly add cold water, in very small amounts at a time, stirring constantly to obtain a smooth paste. Gradually stir in a little of the stock from the pan until the mixture becomes liquid.

Strain the sauce into the soup. Add the vinegar and cook for 15 minutes. Add the potatoes to the soup. As soon as the potatoes are cooked, the soup is ready. Before serving, season to taste and remove the savory.

Note: Put a bowl of thick cream on the table as well as fresh tarragon and vinegar so that each person may season their own soup.

Serves 6–8

Best wishes for the success of your cookery book.

Jacques Santer/Prime Minister, Luxemburg

Cullen Skink

1 Finnan haddock	salt and freshly ground black pepper
about 350 g (12 oz) potatoes, cooked and mashed	600 ml (1 pint) milk
	25 g (1 oz) butter

Skin the haddock, put in a saucepan and add just enough boiling water to cover. Simmer for about 5 minutes or until the fish is cooked.

Remove the haddock, remove the skin and bones and return them to the cooking liquid. Cook for about 30 minutes. Meanwhile, flake the fish.

Strain the fish cooking liquid, return to the pan and add the flaked fish and the milk.

Bring to the boil and whisk in enough mashed potatoes to give a creamy consistency. Season with salt and pepper, stir in the butter and serve hot.

Serves 2   *Richard Wilson/Actor*

Piedmont Roasted Peppers

For this it is essential to use a good, solid, shallow roasting tray
40 × 30 cm (16 × 12) inches: if the sides are too deep, the roasted
vegetables won't get those lovely, nutty, toasted edges.

4 large red peppers (green are not suitable)	**2 garlic cloves**
	75 ml (3 fl oz) Italian extra virgin olive oil
4 medium tomatoes	**freshly ground black pepper**
8 tinned anchovy fillets, drained	**I small bunch fresh basil leaves, to serve**

Pre-heat the oven to 180°C (350°F) mark 4.

Begin by cutting the peppers in half and removing the seeds but leaving
the stalks intact (they're not edible but they do look attractive and they help
the pepper halves to keep their shape). Lay the pepper halves in a lightly
oiled roasting-tray.

Now put the tomatoes in a bowl and pour boiling water over them. Leave
them for 1 minute, then drain them and slip the skins off, using a cloth to
protect your hands. Then cut the tomatoes in quarters and place two quarters
in each pepper half.

After that snip one anchovy fillet per pepper half into rough pieces and
add to the tomatoes. Peel the garlic cloves, slice them thinly and divide the
slices equally among the tomatoes and anchovies.

Spoon 1 dessertspoon of olive oil into each pepper, season with freshly
milled pepper (but no salt because of the anchovies) and place the tray on a
high shelf in the oven for the peppers to roast for 50 minutes–1 hour.

Then transfer the cooked peppers to a serving dish with all the precious
juices poured over, and garnish with a few scattered basil leaves.

These do need good bread to go with them as the juices are sublime.

Serves 4   *Delia Smith/Cookery writer*

Potato Dill Soup

7 large potatoes, diced	600 ml (1 pint) double cream
2 onions, chopped	450 ml (¾ pint) sour cream
bunch of spring onions, chopped	salt and freshly ground black pepper
45–60 ml (3–4 tbsp) chopped fresh dill	chopped fresh dill and parsley, to garnish
25 g (1 oz) butter	

Cook the potatoes and onions in a saucepan of boiling water for 15–20 minutes, until tender. Drain and return to the saucepan.

Add the spring onions, dill, butter and double cream and simmer for 10 minutes.

Stir in half the sour cream and heat gently for 2 minutes. Season with salt and pepper.

Garnish each bowl with a swirl of the remaining sour cream and sprinkle with dill and parsley.

Serves 3–4   *Senator Daniel Patrick Moynihan*

Champ

My great grandmother was Irish and she has passed on to me a great love of potato. This dish will not cost much to make in time or trouble – yet on a winter's night it will kindle the coldest heart.

700 g (1½ lb) potatoes	salt and freshly ground black pepper
10 spring onions, or 2 leeks, chopped	60 ml (4 tbsp) melted butter
150 ml (¼ pint) milk	

Cook the potatoes and mash them. Cook the spring onions or leeks, green part as well as white, in the milk for 5–10 minutes. Drain and keep the milk.

Season the mashed potatoes and add the spring onions or leeks. Beat well together and add enough of the reserved hot milk to make the dish creamy and smooth.

Place the mixture in a deep, warmed dish. Make a well in the middle and pour in the hot melted butter. The potato should be dipped into the pool of butter when serving.

Note: Champ can also be made with chopped parsley, chives, young nettle tops or young green peas. In the latter case, the peas are kept whole and added last. For a supper dish, scrambled eggs are often served in the centre, sprinkled with chopped parsley.

Serves 4   *Jeremy Irons/Actor*

Cured Salmon (Gravlax)

30 ml (2 tbsp) sugar	MUSTARD SAUCE
45 ml (3 tbsp) salt	45 ml (3 tbsp) Dijon mustard
45 ml (3 tbsp) chopped fresh dill	30 ml (2 tbsp) sugar
1 kg (2¼ lb) salmon, filleted	25 ml (5 tsp) wine vinegar
5 ml (1 tsp) ground black pepper	450 ml (¾ pint) olive oil
15 ml (1 tbsp) ground white pepper	15 ml (1 tbsp) chopped fresh dill

Mix together the sugar and salt. Sprinkle the dill on to a large shallow dish followed by the salt and sugar mixture.

Press one of the salmon fillets on top of the mixture, to coat the flesh. Repeat with the second fillet. It is important to ensure that the mixture is spread generously on the insides of both fillets. Press the salmon fillets together, wrap in cling film or foil and put a weight on top.

Store the fish in a cold place for 2 days, turning it twice a day. The fish is now cured.

To make the mustard sauce, whisk together all the ingredients. Unwrap the salmon, carve into thick slices and serve with the cold mustard sauce and warm potatoes in a white sauce with plenty of chopped dill.

Serves 10–12

*Gro Harlem Brundtland/
Prime Minister, Norway*

Leek and Potato Soup

50 g (2 oz) butter	250 g (8 oz) leeks, sliced
2 onions, chopped	5 ml (1 tsp) mixed dried herbs
450 g (1 lb) potatoes, diced	150 ml (¼ pint) natural yoghurt
1.1 litres (2 pints) chicken stock	salt and freshly ground black pepper

Melt the butter in a large saucepan and cook the onions and potatoes for a few minutes.

Add the stock, leeks and herbs. Simmer for 15–20 minutes until the potatoes are tender. Allow to cool for 10 minutes.

Stir in the yoghurt, then purée the soup in a food processor or blender. Season to taste. Serve hot or cold.

Serves 4

Cliff Richard/Singer

Carrot Soup

1.4 litres (2½ pints) chicken stock	salt and freshly ground black pepper
700 g (1½ lb) carrots, sliced	bouquet garni
1 onion, chopped	150 ml (¼ pint) single cream
15 ml (1 tbsp) sugar	

Boil the stock, carrots, onion, sugar, salt and pepper and bouquet garni for 30 minutes.

Leave to cool slightly. Remove the bouquet garni then purée in a food processor or blender.

Add the cream and heat gently but do not boil. Serve.

Serves 6

Thank you for your efforts to promote understanding.

*Anne and David McGaughey/
Presbyterian Church in Ireland*

Huevos a la Flamenco

90 ml (6 tbsp) olive oil	12 slices chorizo (spicy Spanish sausage)
2 potatoes, diced	300 ml (½ pint) passata
2 green peppers, diced	4 eggs
60 ml (4 tbsp) cooked peas	

Put 1 tablespoon of oil in each of four individual ovenproof dishes, about 15 cm (6 inches) in diameter. Heat the remaining oil in a frying pan and cook the potatoes until soft. Remove from the pan.

Add the peppers to the pan and cook until just tender.

Divide the potatoes, peppers and peas among the dishes. Put 3 slices of chorizo into each dish. Divide the passata among the dishes.

Make a hollow in the ingredients and break an egg into each one. Bake at 220°C (425°F) mark 7 for 5–10 minutes, until the egg whites have set.

Serves 4

Archbishop Michael Bowen

Kelburn Mousse

425 g (15 oz) can consommé	10 ml (2 tsp) curry powder
225 g (8 oz) full-fat cream cheese	chopped parsley, to garnish

Put the consommé and cream cheese in a food processor or blender and process for a few minutes. Then add the curry powder and blend again, making sure that the curry powder is well absorbed.

Turn into a soufflé dish and chill overnight. Sprinkle with chopped parsley before serving.

Note: In warm weather or a hot dining room the mousse melts rather quickly so it is best to keep it in the fridge until as late as possible.

Serves 6   *Lady Glasgow*

Savoury Omelette

4 eggs	salt and freshly ground black pepper
15 ml (1 tbsp) plain flour	15 g (½ oz) butter
300 ml (½ pint) milk	1 onion, chopped
15 ml (1 tbsp) chopped fresh parsley	

Beat the eggs. Mix the flour and milk to a smooth paste. Stir in the eggs, parsley and seasoning.

Melt the butter in a frying pan and cook the onion until soft.

Pour in the egg mixture and cook gently until browned underneath and almost set. Cut into pieces, turn and cook until set.

Serves 2   *The Rt. Hon. James Molyneaux/MP*

Anglesey Eggs

6 leeks, sliced	*CHEESE SAUCE*
700 g (1½ lb) potatoes	25 g (1 oz) butter
8 hard-boiled eggs, sliced	25 g (1 oz) plain flour
25 g (1 oz) butter or margarine	300 ml (½ pint) milk
salt and freshly ground black pepper	75 g (3 oz) grated Caerphilly cheese

Cook the leeks in boiling salted water for 10 minutes. (I always microwave leeks and find this is much better – cook on HIGH for 6–8 minutes). Boil and mash the potatoes then add the leeks and butter. Season and mix well.

To make the cheese sauce, heat the butter in a saucepan, add the flour and cook, stirring, for 1 minute. Gradually stir in the milk and cook until thickened. Add most of the cheese and season with salt and pepper.

Arrange the mashed potatoes around the sides of an oval or round ovenproof dish. Put the eggs in the middle. Pour the cheese sauce over and sprinkle the remaining cheese over the top. Bake at 200°C (400°F) mark 6 for 20 minutes. Serve with vegetables or a mixed salad – arddferchog!

Serves 4   *Glenys Kinnock/MEP*

Classic Caesar Salad

1 whole head of cos, or crisp lettuce	*DRESSING*
60 ml (4 tbsp) grated Parmesan cheese per person	1 egg yolk
	15 ml (1 tbsp) Dijon mustard
	salt and freshly ground black pepper
CROUTONS	90 ml (6 tbsp) olive oil
1 slice of white bread per person, cut into small cubes	30 ml (2 tbsp) white wine vinegar
	squeeze of lemon juice
60 ml (4 tbsp) olive oil	
1–2 garlic cloves, finely chopped	

Wash and dry the lettuce and tear into thick pieces. Keep in the refrigerator while you prepare the croûtons and dressing.

To make the croûtons, heat the oil in a frying pan, add the garlic and cook gently for 1 minute. Add the cubes of bread and cook, turning, until golden brown. Remove and drain on kitchen paper.

To make the dressing, mix together the egg yolk, mustard and salt and pepper in a large bowl. Slowly whisk in a little olive oil and then alternate with the vinegar until combined. Add a squeeze of lemon juice to taste.

Toss the lettuce in the dressing, sprinkle over the croûtons and Parmesan cheese and serve.

Serves 2–4   *Natasha Richardson/Actress*

Easy Family Beans

4 rashers streaky bacon	60 ml (4 tbsp) Heinz Tomato Ketchup
½ onion, chopped	30–45 ml (2–3 tbsp) light brown sugar
2 × 420 g (15 oz) cans Heinz beans in tomato sauce or Pork 'N' Beans	5 ml (1 tsp) Worcestershire sauce
	pinch of garlic powder

Heat a frying pan, add the bacon and cook until crisp. Drain on absorbent paper towels and crumble.

Drain most of the fat from the frying pan. Add the onion and cook until soft. Stir in the bacon, beans and remaining ingredients. Simmer, uncovered, for about 15 minutes or until the desired consistency, stirring occasionally.

Serves 6   *A. F. O'Reilly/Chairman, Heinz*

Colcannon

This is my favourite recipe, traditionally eaten in Ireland at Halloween. Leftovers can be fried in hot bacon fat until crisp and brown. Good luck!

900 g (2 lb) potatoes	300 ml (½ pint) milk or single cream
450 g (1 lb) kale or cabbage	pinch of ground mace
2 small leeks or green onion tops, chopped	salt and freshly ground black pepper
	100 g (4 oz) butter

Cook the potatoes in boiling water until tender. Cook the kale or cabbage until tender. Simmer the leeks or onion tops in the milk or cream until soft.

Mash the potatoes well. Add the leeks and milk. Chop the kale or cabbage and mix into the potatoes, beating over a low flame until it is a pale green fluff. Season with mace and salt and pepper.

Pile into a warmed dish and make a well in the centre. Melt the butter, pour into the well and serve.

Serves 6   *Sinead Cusack/Actress*

MAIN COURSES

Tuna Fish Pie

50 g (2 oz) margarine, plus extra for greasing	200 g (7 oz) can tuna (with the sign that it isn't netted), drained
15 ml (1 tbsp) flour	30 ml (2 tbsp) chopped fresh parsley
300 ml (½ pint) milk	3 hard-boiled eggs, roughly chopped
salt and freshly ground black pepper	2 tomatoes, sliced (optional)
50 g (2 oz) Cheddar cheese, grated	450 g (1 lb) mashed potatoes

Grease a high-sided ovenproof dish. Melt the margarine in a saucepan, add the flour and cook, stirring, for 1 minute. Gradually add enough milk to make a thick white sauce. Season with salt and pepper, add the grated cheese and heat until melted.

Add the tuna, parsley and hard-boiled eggs. Mix carefully so as not to mash the mixture and pour into the dish.

Put slices of tomato on top, then the mashed potatoes. Cook at 190°C (375°F) mark 5 for 20–30 minutes. Serve with any vegetable.

Serves 2–3   *The Rt. Hon. Paddy Ashdown/MP*

Fillet of Red Mullet

4 shallots, finely chopped	salt and freshly ground black pepper
30 ml (2 tbsp) finely chopped black olives	4 × 150–175 g (5–6 oz) red mullet, scaled and filleted
30 ml (2 tbsp) finely chopped cooked artichoke hearts	
15 ml (1 tbsp) finely chopped fresh basil	150 ml (¼ pint) olive oil
75 ml (3 fl oz) basil vinegar	8 baby courgettes, blanched

Put the shallots, olives, artichoke hearts, basil and vinegar in a small saucepan and heat gently to warm through. Season to taste.

Cook the red mullet fillets, skin side up, in the olive oil for 3–5 minutes, until just cooked.

Pour the sauce on to four serving plates and arrange the fish on top.

Slice the courgettes lengthwise and fan out the slices. Arrange on each plate and serve.

Serves 4   *Lord Charles Forte*

Mussels – the French way

mussels	375 ml (13 fl oz) cheap white wine
6 garlic cloves, crushed (trust me)	15 ml (1 tbsp) Dijon mustard
6 shallots, chopped	6 bay leaves
25 g (1 oz) butter or margarine	

Buy at least 450 g (1 lb) mussels per person (a friend of mine would eat more than 100!) and soak them in the sink. Discard any open or floating mussels. Re-soak them in cold water, removing the moustache.

Gently cook the garlic and shallots in the margarine or butter.

Add the wine and mustard. When these have been simmered gently, add the mussels. Add the bay leaves. Boil furiously for 1 minute. Remove from the heat and let all the flavours mingle. Discard any mussels that have not opened and serve.

Feargal Quinn/Superquinn

Prawns Malabar

1.4 kg (3 lb) uncooked shell-on prawns	10 ml (2 tsp) wine vinegar
30 ml (2 tbsp) olive oil	15 ml (1 tbsp) chopped fresh basil
	15 ml (1 tbsp) chopped fresh mint
MARINADE	15 ml (1 tbsp) turmeric
5 garlic cloves, finely chopped	salt and freshly ground black pepper
10 ml (2 tsp) cayenne pepper	200 ml (7 fl oz) olive oil

To make the marinade, mix together the garlic, cayenne pepper, vinegar, basil, mint, turmeric, salt and pepper and olive oil.

Shell the prawns, toss in the marinade and leave for 6 hours.

Heat the olive oil in a large frying pan and, when very hot, stir in the prawns and marinade. Cook, stirring, for 5 minutes, until the prawns are pink and just cooked (do not overcook or they will be tough).

Serve on a bed of rice accompanied by a green salad or lightly cooked mixed vegetables.

Serves 8

*Mr and Mrs Chris Patten/
Government House, Hong Kong*

Haddock with a Kick in it

450 g (1 lb) fresh haddock, skinned and cut into chunks	600 ml (1 pint) béchamel sauce
	5 ml (1 tsp) mustard powder
450 g (1 lb) smoked haddock, skinned and cut into chunks	5 ml (1 tsp) curry powder
	30 ml (2 tbsp) double cream
1 onion, sliced	4 hard-boiled quails' eggs, sliced
15 ml (1 tbsp) vegetable oil	50 g (2 oz) Parmesan cheese, grated
400 g (14 oz) can chopped tomatoes	

Cook the haddock pieces in a little milk for 10 minutes, until tender. Drain, reserving the milk. Cook the onion in the oil until soft.

Put the onion, chopped tomatoes and fish in an ovenproof dish.

Make a béchamel sauce using some of the milk used to poach the fish. Add the mustard, curry powder and double cream.

Arrange the eggs on top of the fish mixture. Pour over the sauce and sprinkle with Parmesan cheese. Cook in the oven at 180°C (350°F) mark 4 for 15–20 minutes, until golden.

Serves 4   *Edna O'Brien/Writer*

Kouliabyaka

450 g (1 lb) frozen puff pastry, thawed	2 hard-boiled eggs
225 g (8 oz) cooked salmon	small jar of Danish lumpfish roe
225 g (8 oz) cooked haddock	30 ml (2 tbsp) single cream
225 g (8 oz) cooked long grain rice	beaten egg, to glaze

Roll out the pastry into a large square or rectangle. On one half of the pastry, arrange layers of all the remaining ingredients, leaving the lumpfish roe and cream until the end.

Fold over the pastry to form a parcel. Do a few twirly bits on top with little scraps of pastry and brush with beaten egg. Bake at 220°C (425°F) mark 7 for 20 minutes then at 180°C (350°F) mark 4 for a further 20 minutes.

Serves 6   *Maeve Binchy/Writer*

Salmon Pie

	SAUCE
175–225 g (6–8 oz) salmon (can be 2 salmon steaks)	20 g (¾ oz) cornflour
salt and freshly ground black pepper	15 ml (1 tbsp) single cream
5 ml (1 tsp) chopped fresh dill	300 ml (½ pint) milk
5 ml (1 tsp) chopped fresh parsley	1 bay leaf
25 g (1 oz) butter	pinch of ground mace
dash of lemon juice	salt and freshly ground black pepper
2–3 large potatoes	

Put the salmon on a baking sheet that has been covered with a large piece of foil. Season the fish and sprinkle with the dill and parsley. Dot with half the butter and sprinkle with lemon juice.

Fold the foil over the salmon and seal well. Cook in the oven (on the bottom shelf) at 220°C (425°F) mark 7 for 10–15 minutes, until just cooked.

Meanwhile, boil the potatoes and mash. Set aside.

Unwrap the fish, remove any skin and bones and flake the flesh carefully. Set aside.

To make the sauce, mix the cornflour with the cream. Heat the milk with the bay leaf, mace and salt and pepper. Add the cornflour mixture and heat gently, whisking, until the sauce thickens. Remove the bay leaf.

Put a little of the sauce into an ovenproof dish, then some of the flaked salmon. Add the remaining sauce and the remaining salmon. Top with the mashed potatoes, dot with the remaining butter and put under a hot grill for 5 minutes until golden brown. Remove from the grill and leave to rest.

Reheat at 220°C (425°F) mark 7 for 10 minutes before serving. Serve with vegetables such as leeks, carrots or courgettes.

Serves 2

Frank Williams/ Williams Grand Prix Engineering Ltd.

Warm Liver Salad

Fry some finely sliced lamb's liver in butter. Take out and keep warm. Add slices of avocado, fresh slices of orange and chopped parsley to the pan and shake around the pan. Return the liver pieces to the pan and stir gently. Serve at once, with a nice green salad.

Gay Byrne/TV presenter

Sautéed Trout with Fresh Tarragon

50 g (2 oz) butter	2 small trout, cleaned
generous handful of fresh tarragon leaves, roughly chopped	salt and freshly ground black pepper
	juice of 1 lemon

In a frying pan large enough to hold both fish, melt the butter until nut brown in colour (watch carefully so it does not burn).

Add the tarragon, fish, seasoning and lemon juice and cook the fish on one side for 3½ minutes. Turn the fish gently with two wooden spatulas and cook for 4–5 minutes or until springy when touched and the flesh flakes easily. Remove the fish from the pan.

Insert a sharp knife at the back of the trout's head and run it along the back and underside to expose the backbone. Lift the tail and it will come off in one piece with the head. Place the fillets on plates and pour over the sauce from the pan.

Serves 2   *Senator Daniel Patrick Moynihan*

Baked Trout with Potatoes and Carrots

4 cleaned trout	1 lemon, sliced
100 g (4 oz) butter	450 g (1 lb) new potatoes, scrubbed
sprigs of fresh fennel or dill	225 g (8 oz) carrots, sliced
salt and freshly ground black pepper	

Preheat the oven to 200°C (400°F) mark 6. Place each trout on a piece of buttered foil large enough to wrap the fish. Put a knob of butter and a sprig of fennel or dill inside each fish. Sprinkle with salt and pepper and then wrap whole fennel leaves or dill leaves around each fish.

Top with slices of lemon and seal the foil to form a loose parcel. Put the potatoes in buttered foil; top with a knob of butter and seal. Prepare the carrots in the same way.

Cook all the parcels in the oven for 25–30 minutes. The vegetables may take longer than the fish, so they should be put in the oven 5–10 minutes before the fish.

Serves 4   *Martin McGuinness/Sinn Fein*

Pasta con Sarde

In Sicily, most of the ingredients would be fresh, but this is a very good stand-by using store-cupboard ingredients.

75 ml (5 tbsp) olive oil	2 × 125 g (4½ oz) cans sardines in oil, drained
½ small onion, finely chopped	
2 garlic cloves, finely chopped (optional)	salt and freshly ground black pepper
75 g (3 oz) anchovy fillets	350 g (12 oz) penne or other tubular pasta, or spaghettini
200 g (7 oz) can chopped tomatoes	
25 g (1 oz) sultanas	30 ml (2 tbsp) fennel seeds, crushed (parsley will do but it's not the same)
25 g (1 oz) pine nuts	

Heat the oil in a large frying pan and sauté the onion, garlic and anchovies until soft.

Add the tomatoes, sultanas and pine nuts and cook for 10 minutes. Add the sardines and simmer gently for 5 minutes. Season to taste.

Meanwhile, cook the pasta until al dente (not too soft), drain and add to the sauce. Stir together, add the fennel seeds and serve immediately.

Serves 3–4   *Lady Sainsbury*

Lancashire Hotpot

25 g (1 oz) dripping	4 large potatoes, sliced
900 g (2 lb) best end of neck of lamb, trimmed and cut into small pieces	salt and freshly ground black pepper
	600 ml (1 pint) beef stock
2 large onions, sliced	

Melt the dripping in a frying pan and cook the meat until browned all over.

Put a layer of meat in a heavy casserole, then add a layer of onions and a layer of potatoes, seasoning the layers with salt and pepper. Repeat the layers, finishing with a layer of potatoes, completely covering the top.

Pour the stock down the side of the casserole. It should come right to the top of the potato layer, but if not, top up with water.

Cover and simmer for 2 hours on top of the stove, or cook at 180°C (350°F) mark 4 for 2½ hours. Put under a hot grill to crisp and brown the top layer of potatoes.

Serves 4–6   *The Rt. Hon. The Lord Parkinson*

Chicken with Broccoli

15 ml (1 tbsp) vegetable oil	300 g (10 oz) can condensed mushroom soup
2 onions, chopped	
2 garlic cloves, crushed	300 ml (½ pint) single cream
4 chicken breast fillets, skinned	175 g (6 oz) breadcrumbs
450 g (1 lb) broccoli, blanched	50 g (2 oz) grated cheese

Heat the oil in a flameproof casserole and cook the onions, garlic and chicken until the chicken is lightly browned. Put the broccoli on top.

Mix together the soup and cream and pour into the casserole.

Mix together the breadcrumbs and cheese and sprinkle on top. Cook in the oven at 190°C (375°F) mark 5 for 30 minutes. Serve with baked potatoes.

Serves 4   *Mary O'Rourke/MP*

Game Pie

25 g (1 oz) butter	sprig of thyme
2 partridges or 1 partridge and another small game bird, or 1 pheasant, jointed	1 bay leaf
	600 ml (1 pint) hot chicken or veal stock
1 large onion, chopped	salt and freshly ground black pepper
225 g (8 oz) lean beef or veal, cut into 2.5 cm (1 inch) cubes	2 hard-boiled eggs, sliced
	275 g (10 oz) shortcrust or flaky pasty
2 rashers streaky bacon, cut into strips	beaten egg, to glaze
125 g (4 oz) mushrooms, sliced	

Melt the butter in a large frying pan and cook the birds and onion until lightly browned. Remove and set aside.

Add the beef or veal to the pan and cook until browned.

Arrange the beef or veal in the bottom of a large pie dish. Add the birds, onion, bacon, mushrooms and herbs. Add enough stock to just cover, cover tightly with foil and cook in the oven at 150°C (300°F) mark 2 for about 1 hour, until tender. Remove from the oven and allow to cool.

Remove the thyme sprig and bay leaf. Season to taste. Arrange the hard-boiled eggs on top. Add a little more stock to bring the liquid to within 1 cm (½ inch) of the top of the meat.

Roll out the pastry and cover the pie (decorate with a rose and a few leaves cut from the pastry trimmings). Glaze with beaten egg and bake at 200°C (400°F) mark 6 for 20 minutes, or until the pastry is well browned.

Reduce the heat to 130°C (250°F) mark ½, place the pie lower in the oven and bake for a further 15 minutes. Serve with creamed potatoes, parsnips, a green vegetable and a very good claret if possible.

Serves 6   *Sir Edward Heath*

Chicken Toscana

1.4 kg (3 lb) roasting chicken	salt and freshly ground black pepper
450 ml (¾ pint) water	1 small cucumber
1 onion	100 g (4 oz) mushrooms
1 carrot	10 ml (2 tsp) arrowroot
bouquet garni	15 ml (1 tbsp) chopped fresh chives

Put the chicken in a large saucepan with the water, onion, carrot, bouquet garni and salt and pepper. Bring to the boil and simmer for 45–50 minutes.

Meanwhile, peel the cucumber, cut lengthways into quarters then cut into 5 cm (2 inch) pieces. Blanch and drain. Finely chop the mushrooms.

Strain the stock from the chicken into another pan and boil until reduced to 300 ml (½ pint). Add the mushrooms and simmer for 3 minutes.

Carve the chicken into neat joints and arrange in a serving dish.

Mix the arrowroot with a little stock, add to the pan and stir until thickened. Add the chives and cucumber. Spoon over the chicken and serve at once.

Serves 4

I am delighted to contribute to such a worthy cause.

Eileen Carey/Lambeth Palace

Marinated Barbecued Chicken

4.5 kg (10 lb) chicken portions	5 ml (1 tsp) freshly ground black pepper
225 ml (8 fl oz) vinegar	350 ml (12 fl oz) vegetable oil
30 ml (2 tbsp) Worcestershire sauce	5 ml (1 tsp) chopped garlic
30 ml (2 tbsp) tomato ketchup	60 ml (4 tbsp) chopped onion
10 ml (2 tsp) paprika	10 ml (2 tsp) dry mustard
25 ml (5 tsp) salt	450–750 ml (¾–1¼ pints) dry red wine

Two days before grilling, wash the chicken and place in large non-metallic mixing bowl. Mix together all the remaining ingredients and pour over the chicken. Keep refrigerated for 48 hours, stirring 2 or 3 times a day.

The chicken should be grilled very slowly over the barbecue, for 1–1½ hours, while being constantly basted with the marinade.

Serves 20　　　　　　　　　　　*Lady Almine Shannon*

Jo Manazatti

25 g (1 oz) margarine	2 green peppers, sliced
8 onions, sliced	450 g (1 lb) mature Cheddar cheese, cubed
900 g (2 lb) lean pork fillet, cubed	
1 large jar tomato purée	salt and freshly ground black pepper
450 ml (¾ pint) water	cayenne pepper
350 g (12 oz) mushrooms, sliced	450 g (1 lb) conchiglie pasta
300 g (10 oz) can creamed mushrooms or condensed mushroom soup	50 g (2 oz) mature Cheddar cheese, grated

Melt the margarine in a frying pan and cook the onions and pork until browned. Put into a large mixing bowl. Add all the other ingredients, except the pasta and grated cheese, and stir well.

Cook the pasta in a large saucepan of boiling water for 15 minutes, or according to the packet instructions. Drain and add to the pork mixture.

Put into a large ovenproof casserole, sprinkle with grated cheese and put the lid on. Bake at 180°C (350°F) mark 4 for 1 hour.

Serve with a tossed green salad and garlic bread.

Serves 6   *Michael Fish/Weatherman*

Orange Chicken

25 g (1 oz) margarine, melted	100 g (4 oz) brown sugar
15 ml (1 tbsp) prepared mustard	15 ml (1 tbsp) cornflour
1.8 kg (4 lb) chicken, split down the back	15 ml (1 tbsp) cold water
300 ml (½ pint) fresh orange juice	orange slices, to garnish
30 ml (2 tbsp) grated orange rind	

Mix the melted margarine with the mustard and brush over the chicken. Open up the chicken and put it, skin side down, in a greased roasting tin.

Mix together the orange juice, orange rind and brown sugar and pour over the chicken.

Bake at 220°C (425°F) mark 7 for about 45 minutes, basting frequently, until the chicken is tender. Turn the chicken over for the last 15 minutes of cooking time, to brown and glaze the skin. Remove from the tin and keep warm.

Dissolve the cornflour in the cold water, add to the cooking juices in the tin and cook, stirring, until thickened.

Serve the chicken with the sauce and a garnish of orange slices.

Serves 6   *Ben Busiol/TD, Dail Eireann*

Tutu Chicken

3 potatoes, unpeeled	2 large tomatoes, skinned and chopped
I chicken, cut into pieces	400 g (14 oz) can tomato purée
75 g (3 oz) seasoned flour	15 ml (1 tbsp) curry paste
30 ml (2 tbsp) vegetable oil	5 ml (1 tsp) Tabasco sauce
2 onions, chopped	I chicken stock cube
I green pepper, sliced	about 600 ml (1 pint) water

Boil the potatoes for 10 minutes until half cooked. Peel and slice.

Coat the chicken in the seasoned flour. Heat the oil in a frying pan and cook the chicken until browned all over. Remove from the pan.

Add the onions and green pepper and cook until soft. Add the tomatoes and cook for 1 minute.

Add 4–5 tablespoons of the remaining flour to the pan and cook, stirring, for 1 minute.

Add the tomato purée, curry paste, Tabasco sauce, stock cube and sufficient water to make a good sauce.

Put the chicken pieces in a large casserole, cover with the sliced potatoes and top with the vegetable mixture.

Bake at 150°C (300°F) mark 2 for 40 minutes. Serve with rice and a salad.

Serves 4–6   *Archbishop Desmond Tutu*

Turkey Boobs

15 g (½ oz) butter or 15 ml (1 tbsp) vegetable oil	2 turkey breasts
	150 ml (¼ pint) chicken stock
2 onions, sliced	2–3 tomatoes, skinned and chopped
1–2 garlic cloves, chopped	salt and freshly ground black pepper

Heat the butter or oil in a frying pan and cook the onions and garlic until soft. Place the turkey breasts on top and add the stock. Cover and simmer gently for 15 minutes. Add the tomatoes and salt and pepper and simmer for 5–10 minutes, until the turkey is completely cooked through.

Note: As I never use recipes, I add various herbs and/or spices that I may have at hand, such as lemon juice, ginger, dried or fresh herbs, lovage, thyme, fenugreek, etc. One can also use leeks instead of onions. Serve with brown rice and salad or vegetables.

Serves 2   *Dame Vera Lynn*

Barbecued Chicken

This recipe is for a large quantity of barbecue sauce, but it freezes well.

1.4 kg (3 lb) chicken quarters	175 g (6 oz) sugar
1 large garlic clove, crushed	100 g (4 oz) butter or margarine
5 ml (1 tsp) salt	75 ml (3 fl oz) American mustard or other mild mustard
2.5 ml (½ tsp) freshly ground black pepper	
	2 onions, coarsely chopped
15 ml (1 tbsp) vegetable oil	2.5 ml (½ tsp) each salt and freshly ground black pepper
45 ml (3 tbsp) lemon juice	
	125 ml (4 fl oz) Worcestershire sauce
BARBECUE SAUCE	600 ml (1 pint) tomato ketchup
60 ml (4 tbsp) cider vinegar	125 ml (4 fl oz) lemon juice
600 ml (1 pint) water	cayenne pepper

To make the barbecue sauce, put the vinegar, water, sugar, butter or margarine, mustard, onions and salt and pepper in a saucepan. Bring to the boil and cook gently for 20 minutes or until the onion is tender.

Add the Worcestershire sauce, ketchup, lemon juice and cayenne pepper to taste and simmer for 45 minutes. Taste for seasoning and leave to cool.

Put the chicken, garlic, salt, pepper, oil and lemon juice in a large dish or polythene bag. Turn or shake to coat well.

Cover the dish or seal the bag and refrigerate for 24 hours if possible, turning several times.

When the barbecue coals are ready, place the chicken on the grill, skin side up and brush with the marinade. Cook until well browned. Turn, brush with the barbecue sauce and cook for a total of 25–35 minutes, basting frequently with the barbecue sauce, until the chicken is cooked through.

Serves 6–8   *George and Barbara Bush*

Pork Fillet with Port

900 g (2 lb) pork fillet	15 ml (1 tbsp) soy sauce
30 ml (2 tbsp) vegetable oil	10 ml (2 tsp) plain flour
1 small onion, sliced	450 ml (¾ pint) chicken stock
30 ml (2 tbsp) redcurrant jelly	150 ml (¼ pint) port or red wine
30 ml (2 tbsp) tomato purée	salt and freshly ground black pepper

Cut the pork into 1 cm (½ inch) slices. Heat the oil in a saucepan. Add the meat and cook until lightly browned. Remove from the pan. Add the onion, redcurrant jelly, tomato purée and soy sauce to the pan and cook gently for 2 minutes. Stir in the flour. Remove from the heat and gradually add the stock, stirring until smooth.

Return to the heat and boil, stirring, until the sauce thickens. Add the port and salt and pepper to taste. Return the pork to the pan and cook over a low heat for 15–20 minutes, until cooked through. Serve immediately with rice and vegetables.

Serves 6   *Nigel Mansell/Racing driver*

Stewed Oxtail

1 oxtail, divided at the joints	1 blade of mace
1 large onion, sliced	1.25 ml (¼ tsp) allspice
3 carrots, diced	bouquet garni
3–4 young turnips, diced	salt and freshly ground black pepper
3 cloves	15 ml (1 tbsp) lemon juice

Place the oxtail in a large flameproof casserole and cover with water. Boil for 15 minutes. Remove the scum and drain.

Return the meat to the casserole, add the vegetables, spices, bouquet garni and salt and pepper. Cover with fresh water.

Bring to the boil, cover and simmer for about 2½ hours, until tender. Add the lemon juice and serve with croûtons or snippets of toast.

Note: Oxtail takes a long time to cook so it is best to cook it partially the day before. Another advantage of this is that the fat will have solidified on the top by the next morning and can then be lifted off. This makes the stew less rich and much more digestible.

Serves 4   *The Rt. Hon. Betty Boothroyd/*
House of Commons

Bobotie

15 ml (1 tbsp) vegetable oil	150 ml (¼ pint) beef stock or red wine
1 large onion, chopped	
450 g (1 lb) lean minced beef	*TOPPING*
50 g (2 oz) flaked almonds	20 g (¾ oz) butter
1 apple, peeled, cored and chopped	20 g (¾ oz) plain flour
15 ml (1 tbsp) curry powder	300 ml (½ pint) milk
15 ml (1 tbsp) mango chutney	2 eggs, beaten
40 g (1½ oz) sultanas	salt and freshly ground black pepper
15 ml (1 tbsp) lemon juice	

Heat the oil in a frying pan and cook the onion until transparent. Add the minced beef and cook until browned. Add the almonds, apple, curry powder, chutney, sultanas, lemon juice and stock or wine. Cook for about 5 minutes.

Transfer to a pie dish and bake at 180°C (350°F) mark 4 for 15 minutes.

Meanwhile, to make the topping, melt the butter in a small saucepan, add the flour and cook, stirring, for 1 minute. Stir in the milk, being careful not to let the sauce go lumpy.

Cook gently until the sauce has thickened. Take off the heat and allow to cool slightly before adding the eggs. Season with salt and pepper.

Remove the mince mixture from the oven (it should have formed a slight crust) and pour the sauce over the top. Return to the oven and bake for about 40 minutes until the top is golden. Serve with rice and salad.

Serves 4   *Richard Branson*

Cornish Pasties

450 g (1 lb) stewing steak, cubed	salt and freshly ground black pepper
175 g (6 oz) potatoes, diced	shortcrust pastry made with 400 g
175 g (6 oz) swede, diced	(14 oz) plain flour
1 onion, chopped	25 g (1 oz) butter or margarine
2.5 ml (½ tsp) mixed dried herbs	1 egg, beaten, to glaze

Place the meat, potatoes, swede and onion in a bowl and mix in the herbs and seasoning.

Divide the shortcrust pastry into six equal portions and roll out each piece to a 20 cm (8 inch) circle. Spoon the filling onto one half of each circle and top with a little butter or margarine. Brush the edges of the pastry with water, then fold over and press the edges firmly together to seal.

Place the pasties on a baking sheet. Brush with the beaten egg and bake at 220°C (425°F) mark 7 for 15 minutes. Reduce the heat to 170°C (325°F) mark 3 and cook the pasties for a further hour. Serve warm or cold.

Serves 6   *The late Lord Harold Wilson*

Steak with a Mushroom and Red Wine Sauce

25 g (1 oz) butter	150 ml (¼ pint) beef stock
2–3 onions, sliced	225 ml (8 fl oz) red wine
175 g (6 oz) mushrooms, sliced	300 ml (½ pint) double cream
2–3 garlic cloves, crushed	2 steaks, eg, rump

Heat the butter in a frying pan and soften the onions. Remove from the pan. Add the mushrooms and cook until soft. Add to the onions with the garlic.

In a separate pan, boil the stock and the red wine until reduced and thickened slightly. Add the mushrooms, onions and cream and heat gently to warm through. You may need to add some cornflour to thicken the sauce.

Meanwhile, cook the steaks under a preheated grill for 2–4 minutes per side. Pour over the sauce and serve.

Serves 2

I am delighted to be able to help Children for Change and wish you every success with your publication.

John Bruton/Taoiseach, Eire

Chinese Chop Suey

30 ml (2 tbsp) vegetable oil	6 celery sticks, cut into matchsticks
900 g (2 lb) pork or chicken, cut into strips	450 g (1 lb) bean sprouts
1 onion, sliced	5 ml (1 tsp) salt
450 ml (¾ pint) chicken stock	freshly ground black pepper
15 ml (1 tbsp) cornflour	10 ml (2 tsp) soy sauce
30 ml (2 tbsp) water	1.25 ml (¼ tsp) brown sugar
100 g (4 oz) mushrooms, sliced	chopped parsley, to garnish

Heat the oil in a large saucepan. Add the meat and cook until browned. Add the onion and stock, cover and simmer for 20 minutes.

Combine the cornflour and water, add to the pan and bring to the boil, stirring, until thickened. Add all the remaining ingredients. Simmer gently until the vegetables are cooked yet still crisp.

Garnish with chopped parsley and serve with saffron rice.

Serves 4–6   *Dr. Marjorie Mowlam/MP*

Roast Spiced Duck Breast with Honey and Soy Sauce

2 large, boneless, Barbary duck breasts, about 350 g (12 oz each)	30 ml (2 tbsp) clear honey
	30 ml (2 tbsp) mushroom soy sauce
salt and freshly ground white pepper	15 ml (1 tbsp) tomato ketchup
pinch of cayenne pepper	30 ml (2 tbsp) medium sherry
15 ml (1 tbsp) chopped fresh root ginger	100 ml (3½ fl oz) chicken stock
pinch of dried red chilli flakes	lime juice (optional)

Trim the duck breasts and lightly score the skin with a sharp knife. Season the skin with salt, turn the breasts over and season with salt, pepper and a little cayenne pepper.

Place the duck breasts skin side down in a hot, dry ovenproof frying pan. Cook over a moderate heat for about 5 minutes or until the skin is golden and crisp.

Pour off any excess fat, turn the breasts over and cook for about 1 minute to seal the other side. Turn them back on to their skin sides and place the pan in a preheated oven at 220°C (425°F) mark 7 for about 4 minutes for medium rare, 6 minutes for medium, or 10 minutes for well done.

Remove the duck breasts from the pan and let them rest while you make the sauce.

Pour off any fat left in the pan. Add all the other ingredients and boil for 2 minutes until thick enough to coat the back of a spoon. Add a squeeze of lime juice or more soy sauce if necessary.

Slice the duck breasts thinly and arrange on warm plates. Pour over a little sauce and serve.

Serves 4   *Albert Reynolds/TD, Dail Eireann*

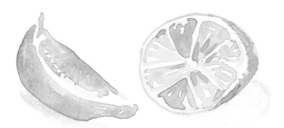

Badminton Chicken (or Turkey)

3.5–4.5 kg (8–10 lb) roasting chicken or turkey, cooked	juice of ½ lemon
	10–15 ml (2–3 tsp) curry powder
600 ml (1 pint) home-made or good quality bought mayonnaise	salt and freshly ground black pepper
	1 fresh mango, peeled and sliced, and sprigs of parsley, to garnish
45 ml (3 tbsp) tomato purée	
175 g (6 oz) mango chutney	

Take all the skin off the bird, remove the bones and cut the meat into bite-size pieces. Use the bones for stock.

Put the mayonnaise, tomato purée, chutney and lemon juice into a bowl, cutting up any large pieces in the chutney. Add 10 ml (2 tsp) curry powder to start and season well with salt and pepper. Taste and add more curry powder if necessary. Add the chicken or turkey, mix well, cover and leave overnight in the refrigerator.

Pile into a shallow serving dish and decorate with mango slices and parsley. Good accompaniments are a rice salad and green salad with fennel.

Serves 12   *The Bishop of Durham*

Spicy Marinated Chicken Breasts

This is an extremely quick and easy dish to make and is quite delicious. It can be made well in advance and left to marinate until you're ready.

4 chicken breasts, boned and skinned	30 ml (2 tbsp) soy sauce
1 onion, chopped	15 ml (1 tbsp) dry sherry
3 garlic cloves, chopped	25 g (1 oz) fresh coriander, finely chopped
2.5 cm (1 inch) piece fresh root ginger, peeled and finely chopped	
	10 ml (2 tsp) clear honey

Cover a baking sheet with enough foil to completely enclose the ingredients. Place the chicken pieces well apart on the foil.

Mix together all the remaining ingredients and spoon over the chicken pieces. Parcel up completely and marinate for 2–6 hours (depending on time available).

Bake at 180°C (350°F) mark 4 for 30 minutes.

Serves 4   *The Rt. Hon. The Baroness Chalker of Wallasey*

The Countess of Shannon's Breakfast Sausage

These sausages are great for a party and taste absolutely wonderful barbecued slowly on an open fire. Omit the vinegar if they are to be frozen.

4.5 kg (10 lb) minced beef	15 g (½ oz) ground coriander
3 kg (6½ lb) minced pork	2.5 ml (½ tsp) ground cloves
75g (3 oz) salt	7.5 ml (½ tbsp) grated nutmeg
freshly ground black pepper	175 ml (6 fl oz) vinegar

Mix together the meats. Mix together the salt and spices and stir in to the meats with the vinegar, working lightly. Let the mixture stand for 30 minutes before stuffing into sausage casings.

Makes about 100 large sausages   *Lady Almine Shannon*

Marinated Kebabs

700–900 g (1½–2 lb) lean lamb, cut into cubes	*MARINADE*
	600 ml (1 pint) sour milk
100–175 g (4–6 oz) mushrooms	2 garlic cloves, crushed
3 rashers bacon, cut into pieces	5 ml (1 tsp) ground ginger
3 tomatoes, halved	5 ml (1 tsp) chilli powder or cayenne pepper
½ lemon	
30 ml (2 tbsp) chopped fresh marjoram	1 very large onion, chopped

Mix together all the marinade ingredients. Add the lamb and leave to marinate for 3–8 hours (the longer the better).

Remove the meat from the marinade. Remove the onion and reserve.

Thread 6 skewers with alternate pieces of meat, mushrooms and bacon, with a tomato half at each end.

Place under a hot grill and cook for about 20 minutes, turning frequently, and basting at each turn with lemon juice and sprinkling with marjoram.

Meanwhile, fry the reserved onions until crisp. Serve the kebabs with plain boiled rice and the fried onions and sprinkle with the rich sauce which will have collected in the grill pan during the cooking.

Serves 3–4   *Sir John Harvey Jones*

Cumberland Sauce

This sauce goes well with sausages, gammon and cold meats. Keep in a covered jar in the refrigerator for up to 1 week.

1 orange	30 ml (2 tbsp) vinegar
1 lemon	pinch of ground ginger
1 small onion or shallot, chopped	cayenne pepper
60 ml (4 tbsp) redcurrant jelly	salt and freshly ground black pepper
10 ml (2 tsp) Dijon mustard	60 ml (4 tbsp) port

Pare very thin strips of rind from the orange and lemon and cut into matchstick strips. Cook in boiling water with the onion or shallot for 5 minutes. Strain the cooking liquid into a bowl.

Squeeze the juice from the orange and lemon. Put into the bowl with the redcurrant jelly, mustard, vinegar, ginger, cayenne pepper and salt and pepper.

Put the bowl over a saucepan of simmering water and heat, stirring all the time, until the jelly has melted and the sauce is smooth (you may have to sieve it if the jelly globules don't dissolve).

Stir in the port and cook for another 5 minutes. Serve cold.

Serves 4   *Lord and Lady Whitelaw*

Spiced Prune Sauce

This is good with ham, pork or turkey; serve hot with hot meats, cold with cold meats. It will keep for a week or more in the refrigerator. Red plums may be substituted for prunes in season.

225–350 g (8–12 oz) prunes	45 ml (3 tbsp) redcurrant jelly
150 ml (¼ pint) red wine	15 ml (1 tbsp) fresh orange juice
1.25 ml (¼ tsp) each ground cinnamon, cloves, nutmeg and ginger	few drops of Tabasco sauce

Put the prunes in a saucepan with the wine and spices and bring to the boil. Simmer, uncovered, for 10 minutes, until the mixture is thick and jammy.

Meanwhile, melt the redcurrant jelly in a bowl over a saucepan of simmering water, then add the orange juice and Tabasco. Stir this into the prunes, mix well and leave to cool.

Serves 4   *Fr Philip Warner*

Ravioli with Feta Cheese and Spinach

30 ml (2 tbsp) olive oil	salt and freshly ground black pepper
I garlic clove, finely chopped	300 g (11 oz) pasta dough
65 g (2½ oz) shallots, finely chopped	I egg, beaten
150 g (5 oz) young leaf spinach, blanched	150 ml (¼ pint) freshly made pesto sauce
200 g (7 oz) feta cheese, crumbled	15 ml (1 tbsp) whipping cream
50 g (2 oz) Parmesan cheese, finely grated	finely grated Sbrinz cheese, toasted pine kernels and diced tomatoes, to serve

Sweat together the olive oil, garlic and shallots for 2–3 minutes without colouring. Remove from the heat.

Place the spinach and feta cheese with the shallot mixture into a food processor or blender and process finely. Add the Parmesan cheese to the processed mixture and season with salt and pepper.

To make the ravioli, divide the pasta dough in two, then roll both pieces thinly to roughly the same size. Brush some of the egg over one piece of the pasta dough and use an 8 cm (3¼ inch) pastry cutter to lightly mark circles on the dough. Pipe or put about 5 ml (1 tsp) of the filling on to each circle.

Lay the second piece of the pasta dough on top and press lightly. Use the pastry cutter to cut through both layers of dough, around the mounds of filling, to make and separate the ravioli. Press the edges together to seal.

Cook the ravioli in a large pan of boiling salted water for about 4–5 minutes, until al dente.

Heat the pesto and whipping cream gently in a large saucepan, then add the ravioli, turning gently for a minute or two.

Divide the ravioli between individual heatproof plates with some of the sauce. Sprinkle with Sbrinz cheese, toasted pine kernels and diced tomatoes, then flash under a hot grill. Serve immediately.

Serves 4–6   *Anton Mosimann/Chef*

Asparagus and Goat's Cheese Tart

PASTRY	15 g (½ oz) unsalted butter
125 g (4½ oz) plain flour	I onion, finely chopped
pinch of salt	10 medium-sized asparagus spears
50 g (2 oz) unsalted butter	125 g (4½ oz) firm goats' cheese
40 g (1½ oz) full-fat cream cheese	3 eggs
I egg yolk	150 ml (¼ pint) double cream
5 ml (I tsp) lemon juice	salt and freshly ground black pepper
5–10 ml (1–2 tsp) iced water	

To make the pastry, sift the flour into a bowl and add the salt. Rub in the butter and cream cheese until thoroughly incorporated.

Lightly beat the egg yolk and add to the bowl with the lemon juice. Mix in, adding enough iced water to bind to a smooth dough. Form the dough into a ball, wrap and chill for 15 minutes.

Turn the dough on to a lightly floured surface and roll it out thinly. Use to line a 20 cm (8 inch) loose-bottomed flan tin or flan ring set on a baking sheet, pressing the dough in gently. Chill for 15 minutes.

Meanwhile, melt the butter in a small frying pan over a low heat and cook the onion until soft and translucent, stirring often. Remove from the heat and leave to cool.

Line the pastry case with baking parchment and weigh down with baking beans or dried beans. Bake at 200°C (400°F) mark 6 for about 20 minutes.

Meanwhile, cook the asparagus spears in boiling salted water for about 6 minutes or until just tender but still firm. Drain well, then refresh briefly in iced water.

Pat dry with absorbent kitchen paper. Cut a 7.5 cm (3 inch) piece from the top end of each spear and cut the stalks into 5 mm (¼ inch) slices.

Remove the pastry case from the oven and remove the beans and paper. Return the pastry case to the oven for 2 minutes. Reduce the oven temperature to 180°C (350°F) mark 4.

Spread the onion over the pastry case. Arrange the asparagus stalks on top. Crumble the cheese and scatter it over the asparagus.

Whisk the eggs and cream together and season with salt and pepper. Pour into the pastry case. Arrange the asparagus tips on top and press down into the egg mixture so they are just showing.

Bake for 30–40 minutes or until golden brown and the filling is set. Serve warm or cold.

Serves 4   *Anton Edelmann/Chef*

Aubergine and Spinach Bake

700–900 g (1½–2 lb) aubergines

plain flour, for coating

60 ml (4 tbsp) vegetable oil

25 g (1 oz) butter or margarine

700–900 g (1½–2 lb) spinach, chopped and washed

50 g (2 oz) grated cheese

CHEESE TOPPING

50 g (2 oz) butter or margarine

1 small onion, chopped

45 ml (3 tbsp) plain flour

450 ml (¾ pint) milk

1.25 ml (¼ tsp) grated nutmeg

pinch of cayenne pepper

salt and freshly ground black pepper

100 g (4 oz) grated cheese

TOMATO NUT SAUCE

45 ml (3 tbsp) vegetable oil

1 onion, chopped

2 garlic cloves, crushed

30 ml (2 tbsp) plain flour (preferably wholemeal)

700 g (1½ lb) tomatoes, peeled and finely chopped or 400 g (14 oz) can chopped tomatoes, drained

1 vegetable stock cube

10 ml (2 tsp) yeast extract

30 ml (2 tbsp) tomato purée

2.5 ml (½ tsp) dried basil

2.5 ml (½ tsp) dried oregano

salt and freshly ground black pepper

1 green or red pepper, sliced

100 g (4 oz) chopped mixed nuts

Trim the aubergines and cut in half lengthways. Put on a greased baking tray, skin-side up and bake at 220°C (425°F) mark 7 for 10–15 minutes.

Leave to cool, then peel and cut lengthways into 1 cm (½ inch) slices. Drain on absorbent kitchen paper and coat with flour. Heat the oil and butter in a large frying pan. Cook the aubergine until golden on both sides.

Put the spinach into a saucepan with only the water that clings to the leaves after washing. Cover and cook for about 10 minutes, until tender.

Meanwhile, make the tomato nut sauce. Heat the oil in a saucepan and cook the onion until transparent. Add the garlic and cook for 30 seconds. Stir in the flour then add the tomatoes, stock cube, yeast extract, tomato purée, herbs and salt and pepper. Bring to the boil, stirring. Simmer for 1 minute. If too thick add water or tomato juice from tin. Add the green pepper and cook until the vegetables are tender. Remove from the heat and stir in the nuts.

To make the cheese topping, heat the butter or margarine in a saucepan, add the onion and cook until transparent. Stir in the flour and cook for 1 minute. Add the milk, nutmeg, cayenne, salt and pepper. Bring to the boil, stirring, until the sauce thickens. Remove from the heat, stir in the cheese and allow to melt. Leave to cool.

Arrange half the aubergine in an ovenproof dish. Cover with half the tomato nut sauce and half the spinach. Repeat the layers. Cover with cheese topping and sprinkle with cheese. Bake at 190°C (375°F) mark 5 for 30–40 minutes.

Serves 4–6

Clare Short/MP

Pasta Florentine

This is a lovely, easy supper or lunch dish for the family – and might, just might, persuade your children to eat spinach! But even if they won't, they'll certainly eat the pasta and sauce.

225 g (8 oz) conchiglie (pasta shells)	300 ml (½ pint) milk
450 g (1 lb) fresh spinach or 225 g (8 oz) frozen leaf spinach (for the lazy)	15 ml (1 tbsp) cornflour
	15 g (½ oz) butter
225 g (8 oz) Ricotta cheese or low-fat cottage cheese	pinch of grated nutmeg
	salt and freshly ground black pepper
15 ml (1 tbsp) olive oil	1 tbsp grated Parmesan cheese

Bring a large saucepan of salted water to the boil, add a little oil just to stop the pasta sticking, and add the pasta. Let it boil for 3 minutes, take it off the heat and put the lid on. Leave it for exactly 7 minutes then drain.

If you are using frozen leaf spinach, defrost it gently, then stir it with the olive oil in a pan over a medium heat until heated through. If you are using fresh spinach, wash it thoroughly, then put it in a pan with the olive oil and let it cook down over a medium heat until it is almost a purée.

Put the spinach in a gratin or baking dish, sprinkle some salt and pepper over it and put the pasta on top. Spoon the Ricotta or cottage cheese on top. If you are using cottage cheese, stir it first with a fork until it is reasonably smooth.

Put the milk and cornflour in a saucepan and mix carefully so it isn't lumpy. Add the butter and bring gently to the boil, stirring, until it thickens into a sauce. Add the nutmeg and salt and pepper, then pour the sauce over the Ricotta or cottage cheese.

Sprinkle the Parmesan cheese over the top and bake at 180°C (350°F) mark 4 or the bottom of an Aga roasting oven for about 20 minutes.

What comes out is a wonderful bubbling layer of golden, cheesey stuff on the top – creamy sauce and creamier cheese – then the pasta and then the green bit of spinach at the bottom.

Serves 4   *Michael Barry/Chef*

The Dalai Lama's Mo Mo's

Mo Mo's are a traditional Tibetan dish – steamed dumplings filled with meat or vegetables, often served with a light soup. They can also be accompanied by a salad of chopped spring onions, tomatoes and cucumber.

FILLING	SOUP
450 g (1 lb) potatoes	30 ml (2 tbsp) olive oil
45 ml (3 tbsp) olive oil	1 onion, chopped
6 onions, chopped	2 tomatoes, skinned and chopped
350 g (12 oz) mushrooms, chopped	15 ml (1 tbsp) chopped fresh coriander
350 g (12 oz) grated cheese	1 vegetable stock cube
bunch of fresh coriander, chopped	450 ml (¾ pint) boiling water
pinch of paprika	
salt and freshly ground black pepper	

DOUGH
450 g (1 lb) plain flour
450–600 ml (¾–1 pint) water

To make the filling, boil and mash the potatoes. Leave to cool.

Heat the olive oil in a saucepan and cook the onions for 5 minutes until soft. Add the mushrooms, cover and cook for 5 minutes or until soft. Leave to cool.

When all the vegetables are cooled, mix with the grated cheese, chopped coriander, paprika and salt and pepper.

To make the dough, mix the flour with enough water to form a smooth dough. Roll out, but not too thinly. Cut into rounds with a 5 cm (2 inch) pastry cutter. Taking each round, press the edges with your thumb and first two fingers, working round the circle. On one side of the round place a tablespoonful of the cooled vegetable mixture, then fold over and press the edges together with either your fingers or a fork, so they are well sealed. Alternatively, hold the round in one hand and, with your thumb and forefinger, gather up the edges into a pleat at the top and press together.

Fill a small steamer with water, first boiling the rack so the dumplings do not stick. Bring the water to the boil. Place the mo mo's in the steamer rack, spacing them well apart as they will expand and stick together if they are too close. Steam for 20 minutes, or until firm and glossy.

To make the soup, heat the olive oil in a saucepan, add the onion and cook until soft. Add the tomatoes and chopped coriander and cook for 5 minutes. Dissolve the stock cube in the boiling water and then add the stock to the pan. Bring to the boil and simmer for 15 minutes. Serve in small bowls as an accompaniment to the dumplings.

Serves 4   *The Dalai Lama*

Savory Nut Roast

1 small onion	30 ml (2 tbsp) wheatgerm or 15 ml (1 tbsp) onion soup mix
25 g (1 oz) butter or vegetable oil	
melted butter or oil for brushing	100 g (4 oz) tomatoes, skinned and sliced or 150 ml (¼ pint) canned tomatoes, drained
50 g (2 oz) walnuts, minced or finely chopped	
50 g (2 oz) cashew nuts, minced or finely chopped	2 eggs
	5 ml (1 tsp) dried mixed herbs or thyme
100 g (4 oz) brazil nuts, minced or finely chopped	salt and freshly ground black pepper

Cook the onion in the butter or oil until soft. Grease an ovenproof dish or loaf tin.

Mix the onion with the remaining ingredients and pack into the dish or loaf tin.

Brush the top with melted butter or oil and bake on the top shelf of the oven at 180°C (350°F) mark 4 for 40 minutes until browned.

Slice and serve hot with gravy or onion sauce, greens and potatoes, or cold with salad, chips or rolls and butter.

Serves 4   *Lord Richard Attenborough*

Pat's Veggie Burgers

100 g (4 oz) mushrooms	175 g (6 oz) wholemeal breadcrumbs
1 onion, chopped	1 egg, beaten
2.5 ml (½ tsp) garlic salt	100 g (4 oz) ground cashew nuts
2.5 ml (½ tsp) celery salt	

Place the mushrooms, onion, garlic salt, celery salt and all but a handful of the breadcrumbs in a food processor. Process until combined and tip into a separate bowl.

Add the egg and nuts and mix together. Divide into four large or eight small portions and shape to form burgers. Dip in the remaining breadcrumbs.

Fry or grill for 4–5 minutes on each side. Serve in a bun with lettuce and mayonnaise or with tomato sauce and vegetables.

Serves 4   *Ken Livingstone/MP*

Vegetable Curry with Turmeric Rice

30–45 ml (2–3 tbsp) vegetable oil

1 small onion, chopped

1 small garlic clove, chopped

450 g (1 lb) diced vegetables, eg, potatoes, carrots, turnips and peas

400 g (14 oz) can chick peas, kidney beans or other beans, drained

5 ml (1 tsp) chilli powder (pick your own strength powder; mild for beginners, hot for the more experienced!)

10 ml (2 tsp) ground coriander

2.5 ml (½ tsp) turmeric

salt

2–3 tomatoes, chopped (canned will do)

15–30 ml (1–2 tbsp) water

TURMERIC RICE

60 ml (4 tbsp) vegetable oil

2 onions, sliced

450 g (1 lb) long grain rice

5 ml (1 tsp) turmeric

900 ml (1½ pints) boiling water

pinch of salt

To make the turmeric rice, heat the oil in a large saucepan, add the onions and fry gently until soft.

Add the rice and turmeric and stir well. Add the water, then bring quickly back to the boil. Cover and cook over a gentle heat until all the liquid has been absorbed (being careful not to stir or lift the lid too much during cooking).

Remove from the heat and leave to stand, still covered, for 15 minutes.

Meanwhile, heat the oil in a large saucepan and gently fry the onion and garlic until light brown.

Add the diced vegetables and chick peas or beans. Stir in the chilli powder, coriander, turmeric and salt to taste. Cook for 2–3 minutes.

Add the tomatoes, stir well and add a little water, if necessary. Cover and cook gently for 10–12 minutes, until the vegetables are just tender and the mixture is dry. Serve with the turmeric rice.

Serves 4   *Patricia McKenna/MP*

Beefless Stroganoff

As a variation to this warming dish, make the sauce without the burgers.
Put the burgers in the bottom of an ovenproof dish and warm through.
Cover with the sauce and serve with rice and green vegetables or a salad.

50 g (2 oz) butter or margarine	6 vegetable burgers, cut into cubes
I large onion, chopped	150 ml (¼ pint) dry white wine
350 g (12 oz) mushrooms, sliced	a little vegetable stock or water
5 ml (I tsp) paprika	75 ml (3 fl oz) sour cream
25 g (I oz) plain flour	2.5 ml (½ tsp) Dijon mustard

Melt the butter or margarine in a saucepan and cook the onion, mushrooms
and paprika for 10 minutes.

Add the flour and the vegetable burgers, stir well and cook for 2 minutes
until browned.

Pour in the wine and simmer very gently for 10–15 minutes, stirring
frequently and adding a little stock or water if the mixture seems dry.

Add the sour cream and mustard and heat gently to warm through: do
not boil or simmer. Serve immediately.

Serves 4–6   *Linda McCartney*

Cheese and Lentil Gratin

15 ml (I tbsp) vegetable oil	100 g (4 oz) grated cheese
I onion, chopped	30 ml (2 tbsp) chopped fresh parsley
I carrot, chopped	I egg, beaten
I celery stick, chopped	salt and freshly ground black pepper
175 g (6 oz) red lentils	30 ml (2 tbsp) wholemeal breadcrumbs
I garlic clove, crushed	30 ml (2 tbsp) sesame seeds
450 ml (¾ pint) water	

Heat the oil in a saucepan, add the onion and cook until soft.

Add the carrot, celery, lentils, garlic and water. Bring to the boil, cover
and simmer for 20 minutes until all the water has been absorbed.

Add three-quarters of the cheese, the parsley and the egg and stir
thoroughly. Season well.

Spoon into a 900 ml (1½ pint) shallow ovenproof dish and smooth the
top. Mix the breadcrumbs with the sesame seeds and the rest of the cheese
and spread over the top.

Bake in a preheated oven at 180°C (350°F) mark 4 for 45 minutes until
the topping is golden brown and crisp. Serve hot with a home-made tomato
sauce or cold with a crisp green salad.

Serves 4   *Joanna Lumley/Actress*

DESSERTS AND BAKING

"The cleverest thing I ever did' said the White Knight to Alice 'was inventing a new pudding during the meat-course."

I have never done that but I did suggest to my London Club that, with frozen fruit, summer pudding could become autumn pudding, and winter pudding and spring pudding, and so it has.

Peter Brooke/MP

Spiced Fruit Squares

450 g (1 lb) dark brown sugar	2.5 ml (½ tsp) ground cinnamon
2 eggs	pinch of allspice
2 egg whites	pinch of ground cloves
30 ml (2 tbsp) clear honey	2.5 ml (½ tsp) salt
5 ml (1 tsp) baking powder	75 g (3 oz) raisins
50 ml (2 fl oz) boiling water	75 g (3 oz) chopped dates
225 g (8 oz) plain flour	50 g (2 oz) walnut pieces

In a large mixing bowl, mix together the brown sugar, eggs and egg whites. Stir in the honey.

Dissolve the baking powder in the boiling water and add to the mixing bowl. Combine the flour and spices and stir into the mixture. Add all the remaining ingredients and stir well.

Grease a 20 × 30 cm (8 × 12 inch) cake tin and pour in the mixture. Bake at 180°C (350°F) mark 4 for 30–40 minutes. To test if cooked, insert a cocktail stick or skewer into the centre of the cake. If it comes out almost dry, the cake is done. Cut into squares while still warm.

Makes 12 squares   *Vice President and Mrs Gore*

Summer Jelly

450 g (1 lb) strawberries	225 g (8 oz) cherries, halved and stoned
450 g (1 lb) raspberries	1 packet strawberry jelly
450 g (1 lb) blackberries	450 ml (¾ pint) boiling water
225 g (8 oz) blueberries	fromage frais or whipped cream, to serve

Wash and prepare all the fruit. Make up the strawberry jelly with the boiling water according to packet instructions. Leave to cool, but not set. Place the strawberries on the bottom of a large glass serving bowl, adding the rest of the fruit in layers and ending with the blackberries.

Pour over the cooled jelly mixture and chill for 4 hours or until set. Serve with fromage frais or whipped cream.

Serves 8

Sir Patrick Mayhew/
Northern Ireland Secretary of State

Fruit Salad

No syrup, light sugar and ice cream – a peaceful harmonious blend.

2 oranges, chopped very small	2 kiwi fruit, chopped very small
2 bananas, chopped very small	20 ml (2 tbsp) sugar
2 apples, chopped very small	ice cream, to serve

Combine all the ingredients. Chill for 1 hour. Serve.

Serves 4–6

Archbishop Worlock

The Countess of Shannon's Dark Fruit Cake

225 g (8 oz) sultanas	5 ml (1 tsp) ground cinnamon
225 g (8 oz) currants	5 ml (1 tsp) ground cloves
450 g (1 lb) dates	5 ml (1 tsp) ground ginger
100 g (4 oz) walnuts, chopped	5 ml (1 tsp) salt
125 ml (4 fl oz) brandy	5 ml (1 tsp) bicarbonate of soda
225 g (8 oz) butter	15 ml (1 tbsp) coffee
100 g (4 oz) sugar	50 g (2 oz) candied peel
4 eggs	100 g (4 oz) glacé cherries
350 g (12 oz) plain flour	225 g (8 oz) marmalade
5 ml (1 tsp) cocoa powder	

Mix together the dried fruit, nuts and brandy and leave for 1 hour.

Beat together the butter and sugar in a large bowl, then add the eggs one by one.

Sift together the flour, cocoa, spices and salt and add to the bowl. Dissolve the bicarbonate of soda in the coffee and add to the bowl with all the remaining ingredients and mix well.

Grease and line a 20 cm (8 inch) square deep cake tin. Pour in the mixture and bake at 150°C (300°F) mark 2 for 4–5 hours.

Note: Brandy can also be poured over the cake after cooking – use about 60 ml (4 tbsp).

Makes 1 × 20 cm (8 inch) square cake   *Lady Almine Shannon*

Lemon Pudding

5 eggs, separated	30 ml (2 tbsp) milk
grated rind and juice of 2 lemons	15 ml (1 tbsp) plain flour
60 ml (4 tbsp, caster sugar	pinch of salt

Whisk the egg whites until firm. Beat the egg yolks and add the lemon rind and juice, caster sugar, milk and lastly the flour and salt.

Lightly fold the egg whites into the mixture and put into an ovenproof dish. Stand the dish in a roasting tin of boiling water and bake at 110°C (225°F) mark ¼ for 30 minutes until the top is browned and the pudding set.

Serves 6   *Sir John Harvey Jones*

My Famous Chocolate Cake

250 g (8 oz) French cooking chocolate	6 eggs, separated
200 g (7 oz) unsalted butter, plus extra for greasing	75 g (3 oz) plain flour
	200 g (7 oz) caster sugar
15 ml (1 tbsp) water	30 ml (2 tbsp) rum (optional)

Preheat oven to 190°C (375°F) mark 5. Very slowly melt the chocolate, butter and water in a large bowl over a saucepan, stirring often. As soon as the mixture is melted, remove from the heat.

Add the egg yolks, one by one, stirring constantly, then add the flour and the sugar.

Beat the egg whites until firm and fold them into the chocolate mixture. Add the rum, if using.

Butter a 20 cm (8 inch) square cake tin and line with baking parchment. Pour in the mixture. Lower the oven temperature to 180°C (350°F) mark 4 and bake the cake for 45 minutes.

Prick with a cocktail stick or skewer to check if it's cooked. If it comes out dry it's OK, if not, cook for a few more minutes, but it's better to slightly undercook it – the cake should be very moist.

Leave to cool slightly then cut it into squares. Serve it on its own or with a crème anglaise.

Note: The cake will rise during cooking and fall again and a light, breakable crust will form on top. It's better to make it the day before and store it in a cake tin. Sometimes I cook it in a well buttered quiche dish and serve it directly from the dish, cutting it like a pie.

Makes 8 squares   *Patsy Puttnam*

Iced Toffee Amaretti Soufflés

12 amaretti biscuits	5 ml (1 tsp) instant coffee dissolved in 5 ml (1 tsp) hot water
6 egg whites	
175 g (6 oz) vanilla sugar	375 ml (12 fl oz) double cream
90 ml (6 tbsp) water	4 toasted almonds
15 ml (1 tbsp) Grand Marnier	icing sugar for dusting

Wrap a baking parchment collar around four small ramekins (standing about 5 cm (2 inches) above the rim). Crush the amaretti biscuits with a rolling pin.

Whisk the the egg whites until stiff. Dissolve the sugar in the water over a gentle heat, bring to the boil and bubble for 3 minutes. Pour the syrup onto the egg whites in a thin stream, whisking constantly at a high speed. Continue to whisk until cool, then add the Grand Marnier and the coffee.

Whip the cream until thick but not stiff, then lightly fold into the mixture. Half fill the ramekins with the soufflé mixture, then sprinkle with about three-quarters of the crushed biscuits. Cover with the remaining soufflé mixture. Freeze for 2 hours, then carefully remove the paper collars.

Coat the sides and tops with the remaining crushed biscuits and place a toasted almond on top of each one. Dust with sifted icing sugar and serve.

Serves 4

I am delighted to enclose my favourite recipe for your book and wish you well in your fund-raising efforts for the children of Northern Ireland. Any help that can be afforded to these children of a divided community is wonderful and hopefully your efforts will make a significant difference.

The Duchess of York

Chestnut Pyramid

This is good enough for a dinner party and provided you haven't lost the tin opener it takes only 5 minutes. It is very rich so portions should be small. Serve with boudoir biscuits.

450 g (1 lb) sweet chestnut pureé	2.5 ml (½ tsp) vanilla essence
100–250 g (4–8 oz) unsalted full-fat cream cheese or curd cheese	100 g (4 oz) dark chocolate, melted or cocoa powder
60 ml (4 tbsp) whipped cream	

Mix the chestnut pureé with the cream cheese according to taste, the whipped cream and vanilla essence. Form it into a pyramid, and then pour over it the melted dark chocolate or sprinkle it with sweet cocoa powder.

Serves 8

Rabbi Lionel Blue

Family Chocolate Cake

175 g (6 oz) margarine or butter	pinch of salt
175 g (6 oz) caster sugar	
3 large eggs	*CHOCOLATE BUTTER CREAM*
50 g (2 oz) cocoa powder	75 g (3 oz) butter
90 ml (6 tbsp) hot water	100 g (4 oz) icing sugar
175 g (6 oz) self-raising flour	50 g (2 oz) dark chocolate, melted
10 ml (2 tsp) baking powder	

Cream together the margarine or butter and sugar. Beat the eggs and gradually add to the creamed mixture.

Mix together the cocoa and hot water and add to the creamed mixture. Fold in the flour, baking powder and salt.

Grease two 18 cm (7 inch) round sandwich tins and divide the mixture between them. Bake at 190°C (375°F) mark 5 for 30 minutes. Turn out on to a wire rack and leave to cool.

To make the chocolate butter cream, cream together the butter and sugar and add the melted chocolate. Use to sandwich together the chocolate cakes.

Makes 8 slices   *Jim Nicholson/MEP*

Apple Charlotte

butter for greasing	15 ml (1 tbsp) grated lemon rind
thin slices of any bread, with crusts removed, buttered on both sides	juice of 1 lemon
	175 g (6 oz) brown sugar
6 large cooking apples, peeled, cored and thinly sliced	apple peel
	whipped cream and ice cream, to serve

Butter a deep square ovenproof dish. Place a layer of bread in the bottom and around the sides. Arrange a layer of apple slices on top. Sprinkle over some of the lemon juice and sugar. Cover with a layer of the buttered bread.

Repeat the layers at least twice, or more if required. Cover with a final layer of the buttered bread. Cover with a layer of apple peel and bake at 185–190°C (350–375°F) mark 4–5 for 45–50 minutes.

Allow to stand for 10 minutes. Remove the apple peel. Turn the charlotte out onto a serving platter and carefully lift off the dish. Sprinkle liberally with icing sugar and decorate the platter with piped cream and serve with a bowl of ice cream balls.

Serves 6   *Paul Keating/Prime Minister, Australia*

Lemon Bars

100 g (4 oz) plain flour	250 g (8 oz) sugar
50 g (2 oz) icing sugar	15 ml (1 tbsp) plain flour
50 g (2 oz) butter or margarine	2.5 ml (½ tsp) baking powder
2 eggs	30 ml (2 tbsp) lemon juice

Mix together the flour, icing sugar and butter or margarine. Pat into a greased 23 cm (9 inch) square cake tin. Bake at 180°C (350°F) mark 4 for 20 minutes.

Mix together the eggs, sugar, flour, baking powder and lemon juice and beat well. Pour over the dough and bake for a further 25 minutes.

Leave to cool. Cut into bars and serve.

Makes 12 bars

This book is a wonderful way to help out those in need.

Senator Patrick Leahy

Apple and Cinnamon Slice

175 g (6 oz) self-raising flour	175 ml (6 fl oz) milk
5 ml (1 tsp) baking powder	3–4 medium-sized eating apples, peeled, cored and thickly sliced
pinch of salt	
100 g (4 oz) caster sugar	2.5 ml (½ tsp) ground cinnamon or mixed spice
100 g (4 oz) butter or margarine	
1 egg, beaten	15 ml (1 tbsp) clear honey, warmed

Grease a 20 cm (8 inch) square cake tin and line with baking parchment. Sift together the flour, baking powder and salt. Stir in the caster sugar and rub in the butter or margarine.

Combine the beaten egg and milk and mix into the flour mixture until it forms a smooth batter. Pour into the tin.

Press the pieces of apple lightly into the batter mixture. Sprinkle the cinnamon or mixed spice over the top and bake at 200°C (400°F) mark 6 for 40–45 minutes, or until the sponge is springy and firm to touch.

Brush the top of the cake with the honey. Remove from the cake tin and serve hot or cold.

Makes 8 slices

Lord Jeffrey Archer

Chocolate and Almond Cake

100 g (4 oz) plain chocolate	pinch of salt
30 ml (2 tbsp) rum or coffee	50 g (2 oz) ground almonds
100 g (4 oz) butter, softened, plus extra for greasing	1.25 ml (¼ tsp) almond essence
100 g (4 oz) caster sugar plus 15 ml (1 tbsp)	50 g (2 oz) sifted plain flour, plus extra for dusting
3 eggs, separated	30 ml (2 tbsp) crème de cacao

Put the chocolate and rum or coffee in a heatproof bowl over a saucepan of simmering water. Heat gently until the chocolate melts. Stir together.

Cream the butter and 100 g (4 oz) sugar for several minutes until they form a pale yellow fluffy mixture. Beat in the egg yolks until well blended.

Whisk the egg whites and salt in a separate bowl until soft peaks are formed. Sprinkle on the remaining 15 ml (1 tbsp) sugar and whisk until stiff peaks are formed.

With a rubber spatula, blend the melted chocolate into the butter, sugar and egg mixture. Stir in the almonds and almond essence.

Fold in a quarter of the egg whites. When partially blended, sift on a quarter of the flour and continue folding in. Continue alternating egg whites and flour until all combined.

Butter and flour a round cake tin 20 cm (8 inches) in diameter and 4 cm (1½ inches) deep. Pour in the mixture and bake at 180°C (350°F) mark 4 for about 35 minutes, until the cake has risen and a skewer inserted into the outer part of the mixture comes out clean, the centre should only move if the tin is shaken and a skewer will come out oily.

Allow the cake to cool for 10 minutes in the tin. Then turn it out onto a wire rack and allow to cool for 1–2 hours.

Prick all over with a fork and spoon over the crème de cacao. Cover the whole cake with butter icing and serve.

Makes 8 slices   *The Duke of Devonshire*

A Busy MP's Home-Made Ice Cream

1.1 litres (2 pints) non-pasteurised Jersey cream	6 ripe (but not discoloured) bananas
	250 g (8 oz) icing sugar

Put all the ingredients in a food processor or blender and purée until smooth.
Pour into a plastic container and put on a lid. Freeze for 3 hours.

Serves 6–8   *Emma Nicholson/MP*

Chairman's Pudding

600 ml (1 pint) milk (full-fat or semi-skimmed)

600 ml (1 pint) whipping cream

4 egg yolks (size 2)

2 eggs (size 2)

25 g (1 oz) caster sugar

90 g (3½ oz) sultanas

small loaf of medium-sliced white bread (approximately 16 slices)

60 g (2½ oz) butter, diced

RASPBERRY SAUCE

200 g (7 oz) raspberries

75 g (3 oz) sugar

60 ml (4 tbsp) red burgundy

strip of pared lemon rind

APRICOT SAUCE

60 ml (4 tbsp) sugar

60 ml (4 tbsp) water

250 g (9 oz) ripe apricots, peeled, halved and stoned

10 ml (2 tsp) lime juice

Pour the milk and cream into a pan and bring to the boil. Remove from the heat. Whisk together the egg yolks, eggs and caster sugar. Stir in the hot milk and cream mixture. Strain into a bowl.

Put half the sultanas into the bottom of a medium-sized ovenproof dish. Remove the crusts from the bread and cut diagonally into quarters. Arrange layers of bread in the dish, dotting with butter.

Pour the egg mixture over the bread and sprinkle with the remaining sultanas.

Place in a deep roasting tin half-filled with warm water. Bake at 150°C (300°F) mark 2 for about 50 minutes or until golden brown.

Meanwhile, make the sauces. Purée the raspberries and press through a sieve. Put the sugar, burgundy and lemon rind in a saucepan and bring to the boil. Add the raspberry purée and boil for about 3–4 minutes. Discard the lemon rind before serving. To make the apricot sauce, put the sugar and water in a saucepan and boil for 3–4 minutes. Leave to cool. Purée the apricots with the sugar syrup then stir in the lime juice. These sauces can be served warm or cold.

To serve, pour the raspberry sauce on to the serving plates, surround it with apricot sauce and place a portion of pudding on top.

Serves 6

I wish you the greatest of good fortune with your splendid project.

Mohamed Al Fayed/Chairman of Harrods

Not So Humble Apple Crumble

550 g (1½ lb) shortcrust pastry	60 g (2½ oz) unsalted butter
2 kg (4½ lb) apples, peeled, cored and cut into wedges	90 g (3½ oz) flour
	60 g (2½ oz) brown sugar
grated rind of 1½ oranges	7.5 ml (1½ tsp) very finely chopped stem ginger
generous pinch of ground cinammon	
3 cloves	fresh berries (eg raspberries and black-
sugar to taste	berries) and whipped cream, to serve

Roll out the pastry and use to line a 25 cm (10 inch) flan tin. Chill for 15 minutes.

Bake at 180°C (350°F) mark 4 for 15–20 minutes. Meanwhile, put the apples in a saucepan with the orange rind, cinnamon and cloves, cover and cook over a gentle heat until the apples are soft, stirring from time to time to stop the apples browning but trying not to break up the apples. Add sugar to taste. Drain off the juices, discard the cloves and leave to cool.

Pack the apples quite firmly into the pastry case. Rub the butter into the flour until it resembles breadcrumbs. Mix in the brown sugar and ginger. Spread the mixture over the top of the apples. Bake at 180°C (350°F) mark 4 for about 25 minutes until golden brown on top.

Serve hot or cold with lots of berries and whipped cream.

Serves 6–8   *The Duchess of Kent*

Gingerbread Men

100 g (4 oz) butter or margarine	15 ml (1 tbsp) black treacle
225 g (8 oz) plain flour	15 ml (1 tbsp) golden syrup
100 g (4 oz) soft brown sugar	5 ml (1 tsp) rum
5 ml (1 tsp) ground ginger	a few currants
25 g (1 oz) candied peel	

Rub the butter into the flour. Stir in the sugar, ground ginger and candied peel. Add the treacle, syrup and rum and mix to a dough with the hands. Cover the bowl and leave in a cool place for at least 1 hour or preferably overnight.

Roll out on a lightly floured surface to a thickness of 2 mm (⅛ inch). Shape into little men, using currants for eyes and buttons. Arrange on a well-greased baking sheet and bake at 190°C (375°F) mark 5 for about 10 minutes until browned. Cool on a wire tray.

Makes about 18   *John and Norma Major*

Sable Aux Fraises

800 g (1¾ lb) strawberries	*PASTRY*
50 g (2 oz) icing sugar	250 g (9 oz) plain flour
	200 g (7 oz) butter, diced
COULIS DE FRUITS	100 g (4 oz) icing sugar
750 g (1 lb 10 oz) sugar	pinch of salt
650 ml (22 fl oz) water	2 egg yolks
90 g (3½ oz) glucose	1 drop of vanilla or lemon essence (optional)
800 g (1¾ lb) fresh fruit (eg strawberries, raspberries, redcurrants, etc)	
30 ml (2 tbsp) lemon juice	

To make the coulis de fruits, put the sugar, water and glucose in a saucepan and bring to the boil, stirring occasionally with a wooden spatula. Boil for about 3 minutes, skimming the surface if necessary.

Pass the syrup through a conical sieve and leave until completely cold before using. Prepare the fruit as appropriate. Place in a blender or food processor with the lemon juice and cooled syrup and process until smooth. Pass through a sieve and chill until required.

To make the pastry, sift the flour on to a work surface and make a well in the centre. Place the butter in the well, then work it with your fingertips until very soft. Sift the icing sugar onto the butter, add the salt and work into the butter. Add the egg yolks and mix well. Gradually draw in the flour and mix until completely amalgamated. Add the vanilla or lemon essence, if using, and rub it into the dough 2 or 3 times with the palm of your hand.

Divide the pastry into two. On a lightly floured surface, roll out both pieces to a thickness of about 2 mm (⅛ inch). Cut out 9 circles from each piece, using a pastry cutter, and arrange them on a baking sheet. Bake at 200°C (400°F) mark 6 for 8 minutes, until golden. Use a palette knife to slide the circles on to a wire rack and leave in a cool place.

Hull the strawberries and cut in half or leave whole, depending on their size. Roll them in two-thirds of the coulis and leave to macerate in the fridge.

To serve, put a pastry circle on each serving plate. Arrange a few macerated strawberries on top, add another pastry circle and more strawberries, and top with a third pastry circle. Sprinkle generously with icing sugar and serve with the remaining coulis.

Serves 6   *Michel Roux/Chef*

Chocolate and Coffee Roulade

250 g (8 oz) good quality dark chocolate	150 g (5 oz) caster sugar
30 ml (2 tbsp) strong black coffee	300 ml (½ pint) double cream
5 large eggs, separated	icing sugar, for dusting

Line a 30 × 35 cm (12 × 14 inch) Swiss roll tin with baking parchment.

Break the chocolate into a heatproof bowl and add the coffee. Put the bowl over a saucepan of simmering water and heat until the chocolate melts. Stir to a thick cream, being careful not to overheat the chocolate. Leave to cool a little.

Whisk the egg yolks, gradually incorporating the caster sugar, until the mixture is very pale and thick. Fold in the melted chocolate.

Whisk the egg whites until they are very stiff, then, using a large metal spoon, fold them quickly and thoroughly into the chocolate mixture. Pour into the Swiss roll tin and bake at 180°C (350°F) mark 4 (bottom right oven in a 4-door Aga) for 20 minutes, or until firm.

Take out of the oven and cover first with a sheet of baking parchment then with a damp tea towel. Leave for several hours or overnight.

To assemble the roulade, remove the tea towel and baking parchment. Lay a fresh sheet of baking parchment on a work surface and dust liberally with sifted icing sugar. Turn the roulade out on to this, and carefully peel the paper off the back.

Whip the cream. Spread the cream over the roulade. Roll up the roulade lengthways and slip it on to a serving dish. Dust with sifted icing sugar and serve.

Serves 6–8   *Sir Peter de la Billière*

Coffee Mousse

30 ml (2 tbsp) water	3 eggs, separated
I packet of gelatine	300 ml (½ pint) whipping cream
50 g (2 oz) caster sugar	30 ml (2 tbsp) coffee essence

Put the water in a small bowl over a saucepan of simmering water. Sprinkle the gelatine over the top. Heat gently until the gelatine has dissolved.

Put the sugar and egg yolks in a bowl over a saucepan of simmering water and whisk together until pale and fluffy. Whisk the egg whites until stiff. Whip the cream until stiff.

Add the coffee and gelatine to the egg yolk mixture. Fold in the cream and egg whites, a little at a time. Pour into a 1 litre (2 pint) soufflé dish and cover with cling film. Chill until set.

Serves 4   *Lady Margaret Thatcher*

Macaroons

100 g (4 oz) ground almonds	75 g (3 oz) icing sugar
1.25 ml (¼ tsp) almond essence	I egg white

Beat together all the ingredients until a smooth dough is formed.

Roll the dough into small balls and bake them on oiled baking parchment at 220°C (425°F) mark 7 for about 6 minutes until they are golden in colour, but still spongy to touch.

Makes about 12   *Lord James Callaghan*

Easy Cheesecake

butter for greasing	450 g (I lb) curd cheese
225 g (8 oz) digestive biscuits	60 ml (4 tbsp) caster sugar
3 eggs	I dessertspoon custard powder mixed
5 ml (I tsp) lemon juice	with a little milk

Butter a 20 cm (8 inch) round cake tin. Crush the biscuits and spread into the tin, pressing down with the back of a spoon.

Gently mix together all the other ingredients and pour on top of the biscuits. Bake at 150°C (300°F) mark 2 for 1 hour. Leave to cool. Chill before serving.

Makes 8 slices   *Maureen Lipman/Writer and actress*

Date and Walnut Loaf

100 g (4 oz) dates, chopped	225 ml (8 fl oz) boiling water
100 g (4 oz) sugar	175 g (6 oz) plain flour, sifted
50 g (2 oz) soft margarine, plus extra for greasing	25 g (I oz) walnuts, chopped
	I egg
5 ml (I tsp) baking soda	few drops of vanilla essence

Put the dates, sugar, margarine and baking soda in a bowl and add the boiling water. Mix well. Add the flour, nuts, egg and vanilla essence and beat well.

Turn into a greased and lined 450 g (1 lb) loaf tin and bake at 180°C (350°F) mark 4 for 1 hour. Cool on a wire rack.

Makes 6–8 slices   *Thelma Mehaffey/Londonderry*

Sunday Special Pudding

450 ml (¾ pint) double cream	**salt**
150 ml (¼ pint) full cream milk	**1 kg (2¼ lb) dessert apples**
1–2 vanilla pods	**25 g (1 oz) butter**
5 large eggs (size 1 or 2), separated	**25 g (1 oz) soft light brown sugar**
10 ml (2 tsp) caster sugar	**250 g (9 oz) caster sugar**

Pour the cream and milk into a large saucepan and stir. Add the vanilla pods, bring to the boil and simmer, stirring, for a moment or two. Then cover the pan and leave until cold, stirring occasionally to mix in any skin that forms. This cooling period allows the vanilla to be infused. When cold, take out the vanilla pods, wash them and leave to dry before storing away again for use another time.

Put the egg yolks into the bowl of an electric mixer and the egg whites in a covered bowl on one side. Add the 10 ml (2 tsp) of caster sugar to the egg yolks with a generous pinch of salt and whisk until pale.

Bring the cream and milk to the boil and pour immediately on to the egg yolk and sugar mixture, whisking all the time. Pour into a large heavy-based saucepan, put over a medium heat and stir constantly for about 10 minutes without letting it quite boil, until you feel the mixture has thickened. Then pour the custard into a wide, ovenproof 1.5–1.75 litre (2¾–3 pint) dish and put on one side.

Now peel the apples, cut out the core and slice into 2.5 cm (1 inch) pieces. Melt the butter in a large, deep frying pan over a high heat. Add the apple pieces and stir around for about 10 minutes until the apples feel soft when you stick a knife through them. Then add the brown sugar and stir for a minute or two until dissolved and toffeeish.

Remove from the heat and leave the apples in the pan for about 10 minutes. Then spoon the apples on to the custard and spoon over the sugar juices.

When you are ready to cook the pudding, heat the oven to 190°C (375°F) mark 5, put the egg whites in a large bowl, add a good pinch of salt and whisk until they form soft peaks. Add all but about 2 tablespoons of the caster sugar and whisk again until they hold peaks. Spoon the meringue on top of the pudding in rough flicks and sprinkle on the remaining sugar. Put the pudding just below the centre of the oven and bake for 12–15 minutes. Serve warm or cold.

Serves 8   *Josceline Dimbleby/Cookery writer*

Semoule Soufflée aux Pommes

My mother used to make this dish when I was a child which made me love her ten times over. It's delicious!

25 g (I oz) butter	**100 g (4 oz) caster sugar**
60 g (2¼ oz) caster sugar	**70 g (2¾ oz) semolina**
4 large ripe eating apples (James Greaves, Junagold or Golden Delicious)	**70 g (2¾ oz) sultanas**
	4 eggs, separated

SEMOLINA SOUFFLE	*TO FINISH THE DISH*
500 ml (18 fl oz) milk	**20 g (¾ oz) unsalted butter**
2 drops vanilla essence or ½ vanilla pod, cut in half and scraped	**caster sugar for sprinkling**

Melt 10 g (¼ oz) of the butter and spread a film of it inside a large shallow ovenproof dish, then sprinkle with 20 g (¾ oz) of the caster sugar. Clean the edge of the dish. Reserve. Preheat the oven to 350°F (180°C) mark 4.

Wash the apples and pat dry. Melt the remaining butter and brush over the apples, then coat with the remaining caster sugar. Place on a buttered baking sheet and bake in the oven for approximately 25–30 minutes, according to ripeness, until tender. Remove from the oven and reserve.

Prepare the semolina soufflé. Bring the milk to the boil together with the vanilla essence or pod, then lower the heat and add 60 g (2¼ oz) of the caster sugar, the semolina and sultanas. Simmer for about 3 minutes until the mixture thickens, whisking all the time to prevent any lumps forming or burning the bottom. Cool for 2–3 minutes, and remove the vanilla pod if used.

In a bowl, whisk the egg whites until soft peaks form, and then slowly add the remaining caster sugar. Continue whisking until stiff peaks have been achieved. Mix the egg yolks into the semolina mixture. Briskly whisk in one-third of the egg white, then fold the remainder in gently with a spatula.

Pour the semolina soufflé mixture into the prepared baking dish and embed the apples in it. Dab a knob of butter on each apple, sprinkle sugar over the dish, and bake in the preheated oven for 25 minutes. Remove the dish from the oven, place it on your table, and let your guests help themselves.

Serves 4   *Raymond Blanc/Chef*

Muskingum Chocolate Dew Cake

This cake is the one our children requested for special occasions such as birthdays. For one who really enjoys chocolate, a chocolate icing on the cake just can't be beaten. Enjoy!

450 g (1 lb) self-raising flour	10 ml (2 tsp) bicarbonate of soda
225 g (8 oz) caster sugar	225 ml (8 fl oz) water
60 ml (4 tbsp) cocoa powder	225 ml (8 fl oz) mayonnaise
2.5 ml (½ tsp) salt	5 ml (1 tsp) vanilla essence

Combine the dry ingredients and sift several times. Combine the water, mayonnaise and vanilla essence and stir in to the dry ingredients. Pour into two greased 20 cm (8 inch) round cake tins and bake at 180°C (350°F) mark 4 for 30 minutes. Test with a skewer or cocktail stick: if it comes out dry, the cake is cooked. Turn out on to a wire rack and leave to cool.

Makes 10–12 slices *Annie Glenn*

Chocolate Mousse

This is an extremely easy recipe to make. It's somewhat expensive but an absolute 'must' for a special dinner party!

4 eggs	200 ml (7 fl oz) double cream
4 egg yolks	20 ml (4 tsp) vanilla essence or 40 ml
2.5 ml (½ tsp) salt	(8 tsp) brandy
350 g (12 oz) plain chocolate, melted	whipped cream, to decorate

Beat the eggs, egg yolks and salt with an electric mixer until fluffy. Add the chocolate and beat until well blended.

Add the cream and vanilla or brandy and beat until the mixture mounds and is smooth. Spoon into a serving bowl or individual dishes. Chill. Decorate with piped whipped cream and serve.

Serves 6–8 *Gloria Hunniford/TV presenter*

Chocolate Sauce

For the easiest, richest, most chocolatey, stickiest chocolate sauce:

Heat 45 ml (3 tbsp) of golden syrup and add 4 dessertspoons of Cadbury's Bourneville Cocoa. Adjust for taste and for toffeeness and pour directly on to ice-cream.

Serves 4   *Dominic Cadbury*

Chocolate Cake

250 g (8 oz) plain chocolate	**6 eggs, separated**
30 ml (2 tbsp) milk	**butter for greasing**
100 g (4 oz) ground almonds	**flour for dusting**
90 ml (6 tbsp) sugar	**caster sugar for sprinkling**

Melt the chocolate with the milk in a double saucepan over boiling water. Mix the melted chocolate with the ground almonds, sugar and egg yolks. Beat well.

Whisk the egg whites until stiff and fold into the chocolate mixture. Butter and flour a 20 cm (8 inch) round cake tin (preferably loose-bottomed) and pour in the mixture. Bake at 180°C (350°F) mark 4 for 45 minutes–1 hour.

Leave to cool, then remove from tin. Sprinkle the top with caster sugar and serve.

Makes 8 slices   *Mrs Terry Waite*

Fruit Dessert

I packet sponge fingers	**300 ml (½ pint) whipping cream, whipped**
400 g (14 oz) can fruit (eg pears, peaches, mixed fruit or raspberries)	**30 ml (2 tbsp) demerara sugar**

Line a flameproof dish with the sponge fingers. Drain the tinned fruit and pour the juices over the sponge fingers. Add whatever fruit is being used.

Cover well with whipped cream, making sure you spread it right to the edges. Chill for a short time.

Just before serving, sprinkle the cream with demerara sugar and place under a hot grill until the sugar caramelizes – this will happen very quickly. Serve immediately.

Serves 4   *Mrs Christine Eames/*
the Archbishop of Armagh's wife

Apple and Hazelnut Strudel

450 g (1 lb) dessert apples, peeled, cored and chopped	3 sheets filo pastry
	40 g (1½ oz) butter, melted
50 g (2 oz) soft brown sugar	100 g (4 oz) hazelnuts, finely chopped and toasted
50 g (2 oz) sultanas	
5 ml (1 tsp) ground cinnamon	icing sugar, for dusting
2.5 ml (½ tsp) grated nutmeg	

Put the apples into a bowl with the sugar, sultanas and spices and mix together until well coated.

Lay a sheet of filo pastry on a work surface and brush with melted butter. Put the remaining two sheets of pastry on top, brushing each one with butter.

Sprinkle on all but 2 tablespoons of the hazelnuts. Turn the apple mixture on to the pastry and spread evenly, leaving a 5 cm (2 inch) border on each long side.

Roll the pastry up from one of the long sides and place on a baking sheet. Brush with butter and sprinkle with the remaining nuts. Bake at 190°C (375°F) mark 5 for 30 minutes until golden brown. Sprinkle with sifted icing sugar and serve warm.

Serves 6   *Lord Rix/Mencap*

Walnut and Date Bread

butter for greasing	75 g (3 oz) stoned dates, chopped
225 g (8 oz) coarse wholemeal flour	100 g (4 oz) glacé cherries
30 ml (2 tbsp) plain white flour	5 ml (1 tsp) bicarbonate of soda
15 ml (1 tbsp) bran	1 egg
15 ml (1 tbsp) wheatgerm	15 ml (1 tbsp) clear honey
15 ml (1 tbsp) oatflakes	300 ml (½ pint) buttermilk
30 ml (2 tbsp) brown sugar	walnut halves and glacé cherries, to decorate
50 g (2 oz) walnuts, chopped	

Grease a 900 g (2 lb) loaf tin. Mix together all the dry ingredients. Whisk together the egg, honey and buttermilk and stir into the dry ingredients. Turn the mixture into the loaf tin and decorate the top with rows of walnut halves and cherries.

Bake at 220°C (425°F) mark 7 for 50 minutes. When done, the bread will have a hollow sound when tapped on the bottom. Cool on a wire rack. Slice and serve.

Makes 8–10 slices   *Professor Brendan Kennelly/*
Trinity College, Dublin

Carrot Cake

225 ml (8 fl oz) vegetable oil, plus extra for greasing	**5 ml (1 tsp) baking soda**
	275 g (10 oz) plain flour
450 g (1 lb) sugar	**350 g (12 oz) carrots, grated**
6 eggs	**grated rind and juice of 1 orange**
100 g (4 oz) walnuts, chopped	
10 ml (2 tsp) vanilla essence	*CREAM CHEESE ICING*
10 ml (2 tsp) baking powder	**225 g (8 oz) cream cheese**
	5 ml (1 tsp) vanilla essence
	225–250 g (8–9 oz) icing sugar

Using an electric mixer at low speed, mix together the oil and sugar and add the eggs, one at a time. Add the nuts and vanilla essence, mixing well.

Sift together the dry ingredients and gradually add to the egg mixture. Add the carrots and orange rind and juice and mix well by hand.

Lightly oil a 23 cm (9 inch) angel cake tin or ring mould and spoon in the mixture. Bake at 190°C (375°F) mark 5 for 5 minutes. Lower the temperature to 180°C (350°F) mark 4 and bake for 1 hour. Turn out on to a wire rack and leave to cool.

To make the icing, mix together all the ingredients and spread onto the cooled cake.

Makes 12 slices   *The Rt. Rev. Dr. Gordon McMullan/*
Bishop of Down and Dromore

Wine Sauce (sweet sauce for puddings)

175 g (6 oz) brown sugar	**40 g (1½ oz) butter**
5 ml (1 tsp) ground cinnamon	**450 ml (¾ pint) water**
30 ml (2 tbsp) plain flour	**50 ml (2 fl oz) red wine**
1 egg	

Mix together all the ingredients except the wine. Cook, stirring, in a double boiler until the sugar has dissolved and the sauce thickens.

Boil for 3 minutes. Remove from the heat and add the red wine. Serve.

Serves 4   *Lady Almine Shannon*

Anita's Orange Tiramisu

3 egg yolks	200 ml (7 fl oz) double cream
100 g (4 oz) caster sugar	300 g (11 oz) mascarpone cheese
grated rind of ½ lemon	4 egg whites
grated rind of ½ orange	16 boudoir biscuits or sponge fingers
60 ml (4 tbsp) orange liqueur	60 ml (4 tbsp) camp coffee
3 leaves of gelatine	cocoa powder for dusting

Put the egg yolks, half the caster sugar and the lemon and orange rinds in a bowl over a saucepan of simmering water and whisk until thick.

Warm the orange liqueur in a small saucepan, add the gelatine and leave to dissolve. Add to the egg and sugar mixture and beat well.

When cold, stir in the cream and the mascarpone. Whisk the egg whites and the remaining caster sugar until stiff and fold in to the mixture.

Soak the boudoir biscuits in the camp coffee for 3–4 minutes.

Arrange a layer of the fingers in a glass serving bowl, followed by a layer of the mascarpone mixture. Repeat the layers until all the ingredients are used up.

Dust the top with sifted cocoa powder and serve with orange segments, marinated in Cointreau.

Serves 4–6   *Paul Gayler/Chef*

Family Fruit Cake

175 g (6 oz) butter or margarine, plus extra for greasing	15 ml (1 tbsp) baking powder
	pinch of salt
175 g (6 oz) caster sugar	350 g (12 oz) mixed dried fruit
3 eggs	60 ml (4 tbsp) milk
175 g (6 oz) plain flour	

Cream together the butter and sugar, then beat in the eggs one at a time.

Sift the flour with the baking powder and salt. Mix with the fruit and add to the creamed mixture with the milk. Mix thoroughly.

Grease and line a 20 cm (8 inch) cake tin. Spoon in the mixture and bake at 170°C (325°F) mark 3 for 1¾–2 hours.

Makes 12 slices   *Rt. Rev. Patrick O'Donoghue*

Eithne O'Brien's Shortbread

225 g (8 oz) plain flour	225 g (8 oz) butter, diced
150 g (5 oz) cornflour	pinch of bicarbonate of soda
100 g (4 oz) icing sugar	caster sugar for sprinkling

Sift the dry ingredients into a mixing bowl. Work the butter into the dry ingredients by hand, until a smooth dough is formed.

Place the dough into a baking tin (Swiss roll shape) and knead down with the knuckles until flat.

Prick the dough with a fork and bake at 170°C (325°F) mark 3 for 1 hour.

Cut into squares, sprinkle liberally with caster sugar and leave to cool.

Makes 12–16 squares   *Bernie Malone/MEP*

Bramble and Apple Jelly

900 g (2 lb) cooking apples	1.7 litres (3 pints) water
900 g (2 lb) blackberries	sugar

Chop the apples into pieces – there's no need to peel and core them. Put in a large pan with the blackberries and water and simmer to a soft pulp.

Pour into a jelly bag and suspend overnight.

Measure the juice and put in a large, heavy-based pan with 450 g (1 lb) of sugar to every 600 ml (1 pint) of juice.

Boil rapidly for 20–30 minutes, spooning off as much scum as possible. You can add 50 g (2 oz) of butter to the boiling juice to help remove the scum, if you like.

Test for setting. Jar and label.

Makes 1.4–1.8 kg (3–4 lb)   *Dr. Marjorie Mowlam/MP*